"Sushil Kumar's book is not only the Bible for small business owners in New York, but also a roadmap to minimize liabilities and maximize rewards. Professional financial advice combined with thought provoking motivational dialogue makes this book a "go-to" resource for running your business with confidence and pride. Thank you, Sushil, for righting my course!"
Glenn Barton, President of Pinwheel Studio Inc., Forest Hills, NY

"Simple, concise, clear about corporation and accounting book that I ever read! I suggest this book to everyone who wants to open business or has a business already"
Tassan Jatikusuma, CEO of Broadway Energy Group & Texnetworks Inc., Queens, NY

"As a fellow New York small business owner, I can say from experience that Sushil Kumar's enlightening and motivational book offers all the key elements to help ensure lasting success."
Lyonel Coriolan, Executive Director & CEO of Emerging Technologies Institute, Forest Hills, NY

"Very informative yet a concise presentation of topics important to any business owner. A must read book for an entry level or a seasoned entrepreneur. Kudos to Mr. Kumar for this excellent resource!"
Robert Niyazov, President of R & J Capital Group Mortgages, LLC, Forest Hills, NY

"This book should be required reading for anyone thinking about starting a business entity or recently started one. It provides solid advice in simple language on how to financially protect yourself, your business and how to financially manage it for future success. It provides real life business answers to real life business questions and concerns of new entrepreneurs. From what type of business entity to establish to how to protect oneself and business financially, to business planning, to accounting and tax compliance needs in one easy read book."
Henry T. Bak, Financial Professional Associate, The Prudential Insurance Company of America

Success in Incorporating Small Businesses

(Twelve Cardinal Steps to Establish a Business in New York)

Trinity Tax & Financial Solutions Inc.

Sushil Kumar, CPA, MBA, CGMA

116-16 Queens Blvd, Suite 245
Forest Hills, NY 11375

T: 718-261-2090
F: 718-261-2185
www.bestcpasolutions.com

authorHOUSE®

AuthorHouse™ LLC
1663 Liberty Drive
Bloomington, IN 47403
www.authorhouse.com
Phone: 1-800-839-8640

Published by AuthorHouse   04/21/2014

ISBN: 978-1-4918-3573-9 (sc)
ISBN: 978-1-4918-3572-2 (e)

This book is dedicated to my teachers, family, clients, and staff, who have all been a blessing to me and inspire me to reach greater heights.

Introduction

Congratulations on your new business.
I wish you every success!

I have written this *Success in Incorporating Small Businesses* to provide you with basic information about the financial, tax, and accounting considerations of starting a new business.

The purpose of this book is twofold. The first is to help you focus on the decision of whether to incorporate and the best way to accomplish it. I personally believe that in business today it is almost a necessity that you be incorporated. I would say this mainly based on the belief that our society has become overly litigious. Those who enter into business must face the fact that sooner or later someone will sue them or their business for something. If you do not have a corporate structure, you will expose yourself and possibly your entire family's assets to the plaintiff in the suit. The corporation is the single most important tool to protect from liability. Incorporation is a great tool from income tax perspective, audit exposure and succession planning.

The second objective of this book is to convey to you the legalities of creating an actual business operation. Operating a business is highly regulated proposition. You have to understand a little about business law to learn to spot potential problems. You may not actually handle the problem yourself, but by understanding some of the legal implications, you will be able to use your accountant and attorney better leverage in dealing with legal tax problems.

Each year hundreds of thousands of corporations are registered in this country, tens of thousands in New York alone.

Many new businesses fail in the early years from poor management and lack of attention to financial basics such as record keeping and reporting. That's where we come in—we want to be part of your team to make sure you have in place the things that will allow you to enjoy ongoing success.

Having a team of outside advisors is important—including a CPA, lawyer, bank manager, and insurance agent. Make sure your advisers are willing to be *engaged* and *proactive* in helping you. You don't need spectators—you need coaches!

Trinity Tax & Financial Solutions Inc. CPAs has been active in the New York area since the 1990s. We specialize in four areas:

1. Helping individuals and families with tax compliance and tax planning.
2. Helping owner-managed businesses with their accounting, tax, and consulting needs so that they can focus on running their businesses.
3. Helping individuals and families with *comprehensive, holistic* wealth management so that they can achieve financial independence and meet their life objectives.
4. Helping expatriate individuals and families with their tax issues. This may involve Americans living abroad or, more often, citizens of other countries living in the United States, either permanently or temporarily on various types of visas. This is a complex area and requires careful planning and compliance.

I would appreciate the opportunity to meet with you either at our office or yours—we are pleased to offer a one-hour complimentary consultation meeting.

Sincerely,

Sushil Kumar

Sushil Kumar, CPA, MBA, CGMA

PS: Call us for a free one-hour initial consultation without obligation.

Please note: While every effort has been made to provide the most up-to-date information, legislation does change. Please contact Sushil Kumar for the latest rates and IRS legislative updates.

Contents

CHAPTER 1
SELECTING A LEGAL ENTITY

Triumph is just a lot of "umph" added to "try."
Marvin Phillips

Selecting a Legal Entity

Congratulations on being in business! One of the first things you will need to decide is what kind of legal entity you are going to use to conduct your activities. The decision depends on the following:

- How you intend to finance your business
- The amount of personal risk you are willing to bear
- Taxation
- Who else is involved—partners, shareholders
- Any legal restrictions
- Exit policy

There are a number of options, which are discussed below. This decision will have a significant impact on the way you are protected under the law and the way you are affected by income tax rules and regulations. Each type of legal entity has its benefits and drawbacks, and each is treated differently for legal and tax purposes.

There are five basic forms of business organizations:

1. Sole Proprietorship

A sole proprietorship is a business owned and operated by an individual or a married couple. It is not considered to be a legal entity in its own right but rather an extension of the individual or individuals who own it. The business owner owns the business assets personally and is responsible for the debts or other liabilities of the business. The income or loss from a sole proprietorship is combined with the other earnings of an individual (or married couple) for income tax purposes.

A sole proprietorship is the simplest form of business to own and operate because it does not require any specific legal organization. It just needs to obtain any required licenses or permits.

2. Partnership

Partnerships can be structured as general partnerships or limited partnerships.

A **general partnership** is comprised of two or more individuals who go into business together. It will

> ### Successful Business Owners
>
> 1. Know what the business will look like in five years
> 2. Have personal objectives in line with the business strategy
> 3. Know their exit plan
> 4. Work *on* their business and not just *in* it

usually file a fictitious business name statement to operate under the partnership name. Each of the individual partners owns the company assets, has responsibility for its liabilities, and has authority to run the business. The authority of the partners and the way in which profits and losses are shared can be established by partnership agreement. Responsibility for liabilities can also be documented in an agreement, but partnership creditors typically have recourse to all the personal assets of each of the partners for settlement of partnership debts.

A **limited partnership** is comprised of one or more general partners and one or more limited partners. Limited partners do not take part in running the business and are not liable for the debts of the partnership. However, if a limited partner does take part in running the business, he or she becomes personally liable. All the general partners are personally liable.

The rights, responsibilities, and obligations of both the limited and general partners are typically detailed in a partnership agreement. Whether you have a limited or general partnership, it is important to have a signed agreement.

4

A partnership is recognized under the law as a legal entity and as such has rights and responsibilities in and of itself. A partnership can enter into contracts, obtain trade credit, and borrow money. Most creditors will require personal guarantees from the general partners when dealing with a small partnership.

A partnership is required to file both federal and state income tax returns. However, a partnership does not generally pay income tax. Partnership income or loss is allocated to the individual partners, and the partners report their shares of the net income or loss on their personal income tax returns.

3. C Corporation

Corporations are regulated by state law, which permits them to function as separate legal entities. A corporation has legal rights and is responsible for the corporation debts and filing income tax returns and paying taxes. Typically, owners or shareholders of a corporation are protected from the liabilities of the business. However, when a corporation is small, creditors may require personal guarantees from the principal owners before extending credit.

The first step is to prepare **articles of incorporation** and **bylaws,** which are then adopted and filed; these govern the rights and obligations of the shareholders, directors, and officers.

Corporations must file annual income tax returns with the IRS and their state's tax agency, as well as other states where they do business. The elections made in a corporation's initial tax returns can have a significant impact on how the business is taxed in the future. Regular corporations (i.e., those that have not elected S status—see below) are referred to as C corporations.

It is advisable to seek the assistance of an experienced lawyer and CPA when incorporating your business, as there are a number of critical decisions to be made that will have far-reaching and long-lasting impact.

4. S Corporation

An S corporation is treated like a regular corporation with one exception—an S corporation pays no income tax. The net income or loss from the S corporation is combined with the other income of the stockholders on their personal tax returns. There are special rules governing the deductibility of S corporation losses, which are generally limited to an individual's tax basis. The tax laws regarding tax basis are quite complex.

S corporation status is attained by filing Form 2553, which must be done in a timely manner. The decision as to whether to elect S status requires appropriate consultation prior to incorporation for new businesses or before filing the election for existing corporations. There are regulations regarding which corporations are eligible to be taxed as S corporations. If a corporation was previously taxed as a C corporation, additional tax considerations may subject the S corporation to a tax liability.

5. Limited Liability Corporation (LLC)

A limited liability corporation (LLC) combines the liability protection of a corporation with the favorable tax treatment of a partnership. If an LLC has two or more members, it can elect to be treated as either a corporation or a partnership for income tax purposes and then files the appropriate tax forms. A single-member LLC can disregard the entity and treat itself as though it were a sole proprietorship.

An LLC is an incorporated business organization that generally protects the owners from individual liability for the organization's obligations and against vicarious liability for the negligence and malfeasance of others. Management may be flexibly structured to allow owners (referred to as members) to apportion management authority as they see fit. Partnership classification is assured under some state statutes and may be attained through proper structuring in others.

Creating an LLC is as simple as forming a corporation. **Articles of organization** must be filed with the secretary of state; they are similar to the articles of incorporation used to form corporations. Filing fees are much the same.

An **operating agreement** defines the rights and obligations of the members, including how profits, losses, and distributions will be shared. Most LLCs will have limitations on the transferability of members' interests and the ability of members to carry on the business after a member ceases to be involved.

Members are generally not liable for the debts and other obligations of the LLC, but they are liable for

- the amounts the members have agreed to contribute to the LLC;
- under some statutes, amounts distributed to the members; and
- any negligence or malfeasance the member individually commits or that the member supervises.

This generally means that members are not liable for the contracts and general liabilities of the LLC or for any mistakes or improper actions of others in the name of the LLC.

One of the major advantages of an LLC is related to tax. If properly structured, it provides the benefit of one level of taxation; as with partnerships, any income generated by the company is passed through to the owners.

6. Fiscal year-end

Four of the five entities that we have described in this chapter will, with rare exceptions, have a December 31 year-end.

The only one that can elect a different year-end is a regular corporation (C corporation). The reasons for electing a noncalendar year-end might include

- matching the natural business cycle of the company,
- delaying the payment of certain taxes, and
- avoiding conflicts with vacations or particularly busy periods.

How we can help

We'll be pleased to assist you with selecting a suitable legal entity and establishing your fiscal year-end.

Buy-Sell Agreements

A buy-sell agreement is a legally binding contract, which requires one party to sell and another party to buy a particular ownership interest in a business in the event of the death or retirement of an owner or upon certain other triggering events, such as disability, divorce, bankruptcy, desire to sell to a third party, or termination. The agreement defines the rights of the parties involved and generally restricts the transfer of stock to an outsider. These agreements are often between co-owners or between the owners and the corporation itself. These agreements may be used for any type of business—corporation, LLC, partnership, etc.

The buy-sell agreement is a separate legal document, which ensures that any ownership transition will occur as planned. To provide the funds needed to make this transition, life or disability insurance must be considered.

This agreement assures the owners of a business that the stocks to their company will not fall into the hands of anyone not connected to the company or without an appropriate interest in running it.

Types of Buy-Sell Agreements

There are two basic types of buy-sell agreements: the stock redemption (or entity purchase) plan and the cross-purchase plan. Each of these serves the same purpose but can have different tax consequences. Further, each can be used with a partnership, corporation, or LLC.

Stock Redemption (or Entity Purchase) Agreement: This agreement is established between the business and the owners. The company itself is the purchaser of the shares of stock in the event of the predetermined triggering events (e.g., death, retirement, disability, divorce, proposed sale to a third party, or bankruptcy).

Cross Purchase Agreement: This agreement is between the owners themselves wherein they agree to personally buy the stock of another owner in the event of the predetermined triggering events.

Advantages and Disadvantages to Consider

Stock Redemption (or Entity Purchase) Agreements
Advantages: Only one life insurance policy on the life of each shareholder is needed to fund the agreement. The premiums are paid by the corporation, and the proceeds would generally be received income tax free, but may be subject to corporate alternative minimum income tax rules (small business corporations with average gross receipts of less than $5,000,000 over a three-year period are exempt from this rule).

Disadvantages: In a C corporation, the company does not receive a step-up basis for the surviving shareholder's interest, and capital gain concerns apply. Further, the C corporation needs to consider the corporate alternative minimum tax rules relative to the receipt of insurance proceeds.

Cross-Purchase Agreements

Advantages: No problem with corporate accumulated earnings tax. The shareholders get a new cost basis for shares purchased, which could save taxes at a later sale. Insurance proceeds would generally be tax free unless shareholders violate transfer for value rules (i.e., if the policy is purchased from its original owner by an ineligible person).

Disadvantages: If the plan or agreement is insured, it could take several insurance policies to cover each shareholder (e.g., if there were three shareholders, six policies would be used) and the premiums on the multiple policies may be unaffordable. Living sellers have a capital gain or loss, but the estate of a deceased shareholder generally recognizes no gain or loss provided the sale price complies with IRS rules. Installment interest paid on a purchase may not be deductible (interest limitation rules may apply).

Checklist for Forming a Corporation or LLC

- ✓ Check the name availability with the state where you will do business.
- ✓ Check the federal trademark name with a trademark attorney.
- ✓ Confer with your CPA to determine the taxation of your entity.
- ✓ Prepare and file articles with the secretary of state and obtain a filing receipt.
- ✓ Publish the articles with a local newspaper of general circulation within your county for an LLC.
- ✓ Prepare bylaws for a corporation.
- ✓ Prepare organizational minutes of the directors or members.
- ✓ Issue stock certificates.
- ✓ Update stock ledger.
- ✓ Obtain a corporate seal.
- ✓ Have an operating and buy/sell agreement for LLC/ corporatios.
- ✓ Obtain federal and state Employer Tax ID numbers.
- ✓ Obtain a sales tax number from the state.
- ✓ Open a bank account in the name of the corporation or LLC.
- ✓ Make up minutes book to maintain records.
- ✓ File S-Corp conversion at federal and state, if necessary.
- ✓ Determine if a small business stock (Sec 1244 of Internal Revenue Service Code).

Comparison of Entities Checklist

Item	Characteristic	Sole Proprietor	Single Member LLCs	C Corp.	S Corp.	Partnership	Multi-Member LLC
	Title	Owner	Member	Shareholder	Shareholder	Partner	Member
1.	Limited Liability	No	Yes	Yes	Yes	No (a)	Yes
2.	Lower audit profile	No	No	No	No	Yes	Yes
3.	Continuity of life (c)	No	No	Yes	Yes	No	Maybe
4.	Centralized management (c)	Yes	Yes	Yes	Yes	Maybe	Maybe
5.	Free transferability of interests (c)	No	No	Yes	Yes	No	Maybe
6.	Number of owners	1	1	1 or more	1-100	2 or more	2 or more
7.	No restrictions on ownership	Yes	Yes	Yes	No	Yes	Yes
8.	Can easily select a fiscal year-end	No	No	Yes	No	No	No
9.	Can deduct 100% of owner's health insurance	Yes	Yes	Yes	Yes	Yes	Yes
10.	Can deduct owner's portion of group term life up to $50,000	No	No	Yes	No	No	No
11.	Able to use lower corporate tax rate	No	No	Yes	No	No	No
12.	Able to compensate an employee with equity	No	No	Yes	Yes	Yes	Yes
13.	Can split income between family members	No	No	Yes	Yes	Yes	Yes
14.	Double tax-earnings, liquidation and IRS audit adjustments	No	No	Yes	No	No	No
15.	Can avoid FICA taxes by Distributions Paying children under 18	No / Yes	No / Yes	No / No	Yes / No	No (a) / Maybe	Maybe / Maybe
16.	Subject to: AMT / PHC and AE tax	Yes / No	Yes / No	Yes / Yes	No / No	No / No	No / No
17.	Able to deduct business loss on individual return	Yes	Yes	No	Yes	Yes	Yes
18.	Can transfer assets 'tax free' where 80% control test is not satisfied	N/A	N/A	No	No	Yes	Yes

Item	Characteristic	Sole Proprietor	Single Member LLC's	C Corp.	S Corp.	Partnership	Multi-Member LLC
	Title	Owner	Member	Shareholder	Shareholder	Partner	Member
19.	Can increase basis by "step-up" election	N/A	N/A	N/A	No	Yes	Yes
20.	Can specially allocate items of income and expense	N/A	N/A	N/A	No	Yes	Yes
21.	Can deduct interest on money borrowed to invest as business interest	Yes	Yes	No	Yes	Yes	Yes
22.	Can use cash basis even if sales > $5,000,000	Yes	Yes	No (b)	Yes	Yes	Yes
23.	Inexpensive to form and maintain	Yes	Yes	No	No	No	No
24.	Able to deduct expenses paid personally in computing AGI	Yes	Yes	No	No	Yes	Yes
25.	Can transfer assets "tax free" where debt > basis	N/A	N/A	No	No	Yes (d)	Yes (d)
26.	Basis for loss includes owner's share of company debt	N/A	N/A	N/A	No	Yes	Yeso
27.	Existence of reliable case law	Yes	No	Yes	Yes	Yes	No
28.	Qualifies for ordinary loss under Section 1244	No	No	Yes	Yes	No	No
29.	May offset active income with passive losses	No	No	Yes	No	No	No
30.	Can easily distribute back the owners investment	Yes	Yes	No	Yes	Yes	Yes
31.	Home office deduction	Yes	Yes	No	No	Yes	Yes
32.	Avoid payroll taxes and administration (if no employees except owner)	Yes	Yes	No	No	Yes	Yes
33.	Can deduct medical costs	Yes (e)	Yes (e)	Yes	No	Yes (e)	Yes (e)

Note: A "Yes" answer suggests a favorable response.
Note: A "No" answer suggests an unfavorable response.

Yes if a limited partner
Except certain farms and PSCs.
See Rev. Proc. 2002-28
Unimportant with check the box Regs.
Yes unless partner basis is zero
Sec. 1051106 health insurance plan

Other considerations:
State Tax Issues
Entities Permitted
Multistate operations
Management Capabilities
Estate Issues
Retirement Issues

CHAPTER 2
REGISTERING WITH THE TAX AUTHORITIES

"By working faithfully eight hours a day you may eventually get to be boss and work twelve hours a day."
Robert Frost

Registering with the Tax Authorities

As a businessperson you will quickly discover that you have extensive tax and information filing requirements with a number of different governmental agencies. Substantial penalties are routinely assessed if the required forms and returns are not properly prepared and filed on a timely basis. Several forms are required when starting a business. While this chapter is not intended to be an all-inclusive list of all filing requirements, it does summarize some of the more common ones. Consult with your legal and accounting professionals to make sure that you meet all the specific filing requirements of your business.

1. Internal Revenue Service

The Internal Revenue Service (IRS) is responsible for collecting federal payroll taxes (including Social Security taxes, federal unemployment taxes, and Medicare taxes) and federal income taxes. All tax forms filed with the IRS require the use of a **Federal Employer Identification Number (FEIN)**. This number is obtained by filing a Form SS-4 by mail, fax, or telephone. It can also be filed online at the IRS website, **www.irs.gov/smallbiz**.

File Form SS-4 early to obtain your FEIN *before* you are required to file tax returns. You can download Form SS-4 and instructions from www.irs.gov/formspubs/.

Payroll tax requirements are detailed in chapter 3. Income tax filing requirements and tax planning are discussed in chapter 4.

2. Department of Taxation and Finance

State Payroll Taxes

The New York State Department of Taxation and Finance (NYSDTF) is responsible for collecting state *payroll* taxes (including state unemployment insurance contributions and state disability insurance contributions) and state income taxes withheld.

To obtain an ER account number, you will need to file Form NYS 100 with the NYS DOL. You may download Form NYS 100 with instructions from www.labor.ny.gov/formsdocs/ui/nys100.

State Income Taxes

The DTF is responsible for collecting state *income* taxes.

All forms filed with DTF require an identification number, which in the case of individuals is his or her Social Security number and in the case of other entities, is the FEIN. Corporations also use their New York corporation number, which is assigned as part of the incorporation process.

> **Successful Business Owners**
>
> 1. Are totally dedicated to their customers
> 2. Know about customer loyalty and retention
> 3. Know their position in the market
> 4. Have a unique selling point that everyone knows about
> 5. Have a strategy to achieve this

State and Local and Sales and Use Tax

The Department of Taxation and Finance (DTF) is responsible for collecting state and local and sales and use tax.

If you sell or lease merchandise, vehicles, or other tangible personal property in New York, then you need a Certificate of Authority. A seller's license allows you to sell at the wholesale or retail level.

To obtain a Certificate of Authority, you will file Form DTF-17 with the DTF. There is no fee for the license (and permit number), but you will likely be required to renew it once in two years.

A blank Form DTF-17 with instructions can be downloaded from http://www.tax.ny.gov/bus/ads/webdtf17.htm.

3. Business License

Obtain a business license from the city in which your business is located. Applications can be obtained from city hall or in some cases online. Registration requirements can be obtained from this link www.dos.ny.gov/licensing.

The fee for a business license can range from $25 to $25,000, depending on the city and the size of the business. Your business license must generally be renewed annually. Business in New York City can be registered at NYC Business Express at www.nyc.gov/bizexpress

4. Tax Calendar

Significant filing dates for a corporation using a calendar year-end are summarized as follows:

DATE	RETURNS
January 31	Payroll tax returns. Annual Form W-2s issued to employees. Form 1099s issued to payees.
February 28	Form W-2s/W-3s filed with Social Security Administration. Form 1099s and 1096s filed with IRS.
March 15	Corporate income tax returns. S-Corp conversion for calendar year corporations.
March 20	Sales tax returns.

April 15	Estimated income tax payments. Individual income tax returns. Partnership and LLC income tax returns.
April 30	Quarterly payroll tax returns.
June 15	Estimated income tax payments.
June 20	Sales tax returns.
July 31	Quarterly payroll tax returns.
September 15	Estimated income tax payments. Partnership and LLC income tax returns on extension. Corporate income tax returns on extension.
September 20	Sales tax returns.
October 15	Individual income tax returns on extension.
October 31	Quarterly payroll tax returns.
November-December	Year-end tax planning.
December 20	Sales tax returns.
January 15	Estimated income tax payments.

Note: Many of these requirements also apply to partnerships and sole proprietorships. When a year-end other than December 31 is used (see chapter 5) some of these dates will vary.

When dealing in certain regulated industries, such as utilities or petroleum, there are also numerous other tax filing deadlines of importance.

* Larger companies may have to file sales tax returns on a monthly, quarterly, or semiannual basis.

How we can help

Please call us, and we'll help you register with the various tax authorities.

CHAPTER 3
TRADEMARKS AND COPYRIGHTS

"There can be no rainbow without
a cloud and a storm."
John Heyl Vincent

Trademarks and Copyrights

It is important that the trademarks and trade names of a business be protected. Protecting them may be a complicated process. An attorney should be consulted to ensure proper protection.

When a business is being incorporated, the early focus is usually on choosing the corporate name. But how important is it to pay attention to trademarks and trade names as well at the time of incorporation? If one cares about controlling unbudgeted expenses and losses, the answer is that it's very important.

Here are the primary reasons why:

> ### Successful Business Owners
>
> Swarm themselves with friends who are accountants, business coaches, and financial planners

The use of a corporate name, even if used strictly as a corporate name, can still violate rights others may already have in trademarks, service marks, and trade names. Hence, even if the state authorities say it is okay to use a particular proposed corporate name, this does not insulate you from liability for an infringement claim from third parties. Generally, if someone has prior rights in a mark or name, and if your new corporate name would cause a likely confusion with that prior name or mark, that would constitute infringement. Therefore, it is always wise to search any proposed corporate name defensively for any existing *federal trademark and service mark registrations, and* state trademark and trade name registrations, as well as common law rights, before initiating use. Federal registrations are particularly important because federal law is supreme and trumps any rights one obtains at a state level. If there is already a federal trademark registration out there for the same or a confusingly similar word or words as the ones you intend to use for a corporate name, then you are risking a challenge by adopting that name.

Some companies choose to use a variation of their name for products (trademark), services (service mark), and as a division name or as an alternate business name (trade name). However, such uses may bring a company into conflict with others who are already using the same or a confusingly similar name for the same or related products, or for the same or related services. Hence, an increasingly diversified company that starts in one area may use "Baloney Inc." as its corporate name and "Baloney" as its principal mark for balloons without problems. But when the company expands its use of Baloney to outdoor recreational equipment, it may find that someone is already using that mark. This means that a company should not merely search for availability of a corporate name but should consider whether or not projected uses of the corporate name as marks or trade names might be impacted by what is already out there.

Searching for potential conflict now or in the future is a strategic art and is not a rote science. Hiring an experienced intellectual property attorney with **good judgment** to perform and analyze these searches is a priority for all new and sophisticated companies. When adopting a corporate name, a company and its counsel must go beyond the simple issue of whether or not a proposed name is available in any particular state. Instead, one should think more broadly in order to avoid being sued later for trademark or trade name infringement, and to arrive at a protectable name.

In summary, when selecting a corporate name, or derivations thereof, you should conduct a thorough search.

By going beyond state corporate records, you immediately increase your chances for commercial success.

How we can help

We can refer you to some good attorneys to do the trademark search and register the same.

CHAPTER 4
BANKING

"You cannot change your destination overnight,
but you can change your direction overnight."
Jim Rohn

CHAPTER 4
Banking

As a business owner, the next step is to open a bank account.

Types of Banks:

Commercial banks offer accounts and loans to business but also to people like you. They are insured by the FDIC.

Credit unions are owned by the people who use them. You have to be a member to use a credit union. Whether you can be a member depends on where you live, work, or go to school. You usually have to pay a one-time fee to join. Credit unions are insured by National Credit Union Administration (NCUA). You earn dividends on the money you put in your account, which is the same as earning interest.

Savings banks pay interest on the money you put in. They may also offer other services and products. They are also insured by the FDIC.

Savings and loans pay interest on the money you put in and offer loans, usually for homes. They may also offer other services and products. They are insured by the FDIC.

Internet banks let you open savings and in some cases, checking, accounts online.
They do not have an office you can go to. You need a computer to get on the Internet. Before opening an Internet account, you should make sure that the bank is a safe place for your money. You should check out with the Division of Consumer Affairs.

Type of Accounts

Checking: A checking account lets you put your money in the bank (deposit) and lets you take out by writing personal checks, using ATMs, debit cards, or getting it from a bank teller.

Some banks charge fees to keep checking accounts and to use ATMs or debit cards. When you deposit a check, it may take several days before you can get the money out of the bank. This depends on many things, including whether the deposited check is from a local bank. The quickest way to get your money is to have your paycheck, pension, or any other money put into your account electronically. A direct deposit facilitates efficient credit into your account.

Savings: This type of account generally earns interest on the money you deposit. A statement account will entitle you to a monthly statement. Federal law allows you to take out or transfer money only six times a month. This account is not used to pay bills. Interest is based on the (APY) annual percentage yield.

Opening a bank account

You can open an account at a local bank office or on the bank's website. The law requires that banks ask for your name, date of birth, address, and an identification number such as a passport or Social Security number. You will need the following at least to open a personal bank account:

Successful Business Owners

1. Open a business checking and an overdraft line of credit
2. Order bank statements on a calendar month basis
3. Request one copy of bank statements to be sent to their accountant
4. Apply for merchant banking and a corporate credit card from the same bank to get the best rates

---

- Driver's license or a passport or a green card
- Social Security card
- Proof of address (utility bill)

If you are not a citizen or a resident of the United States and you do not have a Social Security card, banks are likely to ask you for the following:

- Individual Taxpayer Identification Number: a number given by the Internal Revenue Service for people who do not have a Social Security number
- Foreign government-issued ID with a photo (passport or consular ID)
- Alien ID card

If you own a business, then you should open a business bank account (separate from personal bank account). From the Internal Revenue Service this is mandatory. The business owner must keep the business transaction separate from the personal transaction. Comingling of funds will lead to "piercing the corporate veil," which in effect means that the corporation does not exist and the protection of limited liability is terminated.

The banks will normally ask for the following documentation:

- Filing receipt issued by New York State
- Employer Tax Identification Number issued by the Internal Revenue Service
- Corporate seal
- Driver's license

How we can help

We can assist you to get in touch with some of the local banks.

We can help you get an Individual Tax Identification Number.

Questions to Ask Your Bank

- ✓ Do you give an overdraft line of credit to link it to checking to protect bounced checks?
- ✓ How much money do I need to open a checking account?
- ✓ What is the lowest amount of money I need to keep in my account to avoid being charged a fee?
- ✓ Do I have to pay a fee for every month for keeping this account?
- ✓ What are the fees for using the overdraft or for bounced checks?
- ✓ Are there fees for using the debit card or ATM?
  - ◆ With the same bank?
  - ◆ With any other bank?

- ✓ Do you have a branch where I live or where I work?
- ✓ How long does it take to clear a check when I deposit a check?
- ✓ Does the checking account pay interest?
- ✓ Can you set up my account for online access?
- ✓ Can I use an online account to transfer money or pay bills?
- ✓ Can I get canceled checks back?
- ✓ How many checks can be written before fees are charged?

- ✓ Do you offer loan, money order, and wire transfer services?

CHAPTER 5

FEDERAL AND STATE PAYROLL TAXES

If you are not financially independent by the time you are fifty, it doesn't mean you are living in the wrong country or at the wrong time. It simply means that you have the wrong plan.

CHAPTER 5
Federal and State Payroll Taxes

If you have employees, you will be responsible for collecting payroll taxes and filing payroll tax reports.

Failure to deposit payroll taxes in a timely manner results in substantial penalties and interest. New businesses frequently get into trouble because they do not follow the strict payroll tax rules. Be sure to consult your tax adviser ***before*** hiring employees. Decide who will be responsible for the payroll process, preparing the checks, depositing payroll taxes, and preparing payroll reports. Because of the complexities involved, most businesses use a payroll service.

1. Federal Payroll Taxes

The following chart contains tax rates and the taxable wage basis for employers and employees. Please contact our office for the most up-to-date information.

Social Security Tax (FICA) and Federal Unemployment Tax (FUTA)

	Medicare	Soc. Sec.	Total
FICA tax rate for employer	1.45%	6.2%	7.65%
FICA tax rate for employee	1.45%	6.2%	7.65%
On wages not to exceed	No Limit	$ 110,100	
Maximum employer contribution	No Limit	$ 8,170	
Federal Unemployment Tax (employer only): gross federal tax rate			6.2%
Less credit for New York Unemployment Insurance			5.4%
Net FUTA rate			0.8%
On wages not to exceed			$7,000
Maximum employer contribution (per employee)			$56

In addition to the above federal payroll taxes, you are required as an employer to withhold federal income taxes from each employee according to the number of exemptions claimed.

2. Federal Payroll Tax Deposit Requirements

The deposit requirements for employer *and* employee portions of Social Security taxes (FICA) and federal income tax withheld (FITW) are as follows:

Look-back period. Your deposit schedule for a calendar year is determined from the total taxes reported on your Forms 941, in a four-quarter look-back period. The look-back period begins July 1 and ends June 30 of the prior year. If you reported $50,000 or less of taxes for the look-back period, you are a monthly schedule depositor; if you reported more than $50,000, you are a semiweekly schedule depositor.

New employers. During the first calendar year of business, the tax liability for each quarter in the look-back period is considered to be zero. Therefore, you are a monthly schedule depositor for the first calendar year of business. However, see the one-day depositor rule below.

1. **Monthly Depositor.** An employer that reported employment taxes of $50,000 or less during the look-back period generally must make only monthly deposits for the entire calendar year. The deposit for a month must be made on or before the fifteenth day of the following month.

2. **Semiweekly Wednesday/Friday Depositor**. An employer that reported employment taxes of more than $50,000 during the look-back period is a semiweekly depositor for the entire year. Such employers must make deposits on or before Wednesdays or Fridays depending on the timing

of their payrolls. Specifically, employment taxes from payments to employees made on Wednesdays, Thursdays, or Fridays must be deposited on or before the following Wednesday. Taxes from Saturday, Sunday, Monday, or Tuesday payments to employees must be deposited by the following Friday.

3. **Nonbanking Days.** Semiweekly depositors have at least three banking days to make a deposit. If any of the three weekdays following the close of a semiweekly period is a bank holiday, the employer will have an additional banking day to make the deposit. For example, if Monday is a bank holiday, deposits from the prior week Wednesday through Friday period can be made by the following Thursday, rather than by the regular Wednesday deposit day.

---

5 Great Marketing Questions

Q. Why did we start this business?
Q. Where do our/will our first customers come from?
Q. Why do/will our customers buy from us?
Q. What is our single greatest advantage over the competition?
Q. What is our unique selling proposition?

---

4. **One-Day Depositor.** If a monthly or semiweekly depositor accumulates employment taxes of $100,000 or more during a deposit period (monthly or semiweekly), it must deposit the taxes by the next banking day. This rule overrides the normal rules for determining deposit dates discussed above. A monthly depositor that must make a one-day deposit under this rule immediately becomes a semiweekly depositor **for the rest of the calendar year *and* the following year.**

3. Federal Unemployment Taxes

To determine your quarterly liability for FUTA, multiply by .008 that part of the first $7,000 of each employee's annual wages that you paid during the quarter. If the resultant liability for all employees for the quarter is $100 or less, there is no requirement to deposit it currently, you merely add it to your liability for the following quarter.

If your liability for any calendar quarter (plus any undeposited taxes for an earlier quarter) is more than $500, you are required to deposit the taxes by the end of the following month.

If the tax reported on your annual federal unemployment tax return, Form 940, less deposits for the year is:

1. **More than $500,** you must deposit by the last day of January.
2. **Less than $500,** you may pay the taxes when you file Form 940.

4. Supplemental Wages

If supplemental wages—such as bonuses, commissions, and overtime pay—are included in the same payment with regular wages, tax to be withheld is determined as if the total of the supplemental and regular wages was a single payment for the regular payroll period.

If supplemental wages are not paid with the same payment as the regular wages, the employer may

1. withhold at a flat rate of 25 percent for federal and 9 percent for New York;

2. combine the supplemental wage with the last regular wage, determine the tax on the total wage, and then subtract the amounts already withheld on the regular wage payment.

5. Fringe Benefits

Gross income does not include fringe benefits that qualify for exclusion, as described in the categories listed below. Fringe benefits that qualify for the exclusion are exempt from income tax and Social Security tax withholding. Conversely, benefits that do **not** qualify are subject to these taxes. An example of a common nonqualifying benefit subject to tax is the automobile allowance.

No-additional-cost service. Some services to an employee are excludable if (1) they are offered for sale to the public in the ordinary course of the employer's line of business in which the employee works, and (2) the employer does not incur substantial additional cost. For example, employers who furnish airline travel or hotel rooms to employees working in these lines of businesses in such ways that nonemployee customers are not displaced and employers incur no substantial additional cost can exclude the cost of the room or travel from the employee's gross income.

Qualified employee discount. Any employee discount is an excludable qualified employee discount if: (1) in the case of property, it does not exceed the gross profit percentage of the price at which the property is being offered to customers; (2) in the case of a service, it does not exceed 20 percent of the price at which the service is being offered.

Working condition fringe. Any employer-provided property or services are excludable benefits to the extent that they are deductible as ordinary and necessary business expense had the employee paid for them. Under certain conditions, the fair market value of a qualified demonstration automobile used by a full-time auto salesperson is an excludable working condition fringe.

De minimis fringe. Property or services not otherwise tax-free are excludable if their value is so small as to make accounting unreasonable or administratively impractical. An operation of any eating facility for employees is an excludable de minimis fringe if it is located on or near the employer's business premises and the revenue derived normally equals or exceeds the direct operating costs of the facility.

Qualified Moving Expenses Reimbursement. An employee may exclude from gross income an amount received from an employer for payment of qualified moving expenses.

Transportation Fringe Benefits. An employee may exclude from gross income certain maximum amounts received from an employer as reimbursements for transit passes, vanpooling expenses, and qualified parking expenses.

6. Other Tax Requirements

Whenever a wage payment is made, the employer must provide the employee with a statement of gross wages and specific deductions (if any). Use the Form W-4 submitted by the employee and the tax tables provided in the employer's tax guides to determine the correct income tax to withhold. If the employee fails to submit a Form W-4, the employer must withhold at the rate applicable to a single person who has no withholding exemptions. Employers must submit, with their quarterly payroll tax returns, a copy of any Form W-4 on which an employee is claiming the equivalent of ten or more withholding exemptions.

An employer must also complete a Form I-9 for each employee and obtain the necessary documentation to verify eligibility status.

When making a reimbursement or payment of moving expenses to an employee, the employer must complete and furnish the employee with a Form 4782.

An employer must furnish a Form W-2 to each employee showing remuneration and withheld taxes for each calendar year. Flat-rate expense account allowance, disability insurance paid by the employer, and moving expense reimbursements are among the items to be included as other compensation on a Form W-2. Upon request, a Form W-2 must be furnished to a terminated employee within thirty days after the request or the final wage payment, whichever is later. All other Forms W-2 should be given to the employees by January 31 of the following year.

7. Available Publications

Circular E, Publication 15, Employer's Tax Guide, which covers the payroll tax reporting and deposit requirements, is available at the local office of the Internal Revenue Service or on the IRS website, www.irs.gov. Search the website by using the keyword "Publication 15."

8. New York State Payroll Taxes

The following chart contains tax rates and the taxable wage basis for employers and employees. The limits and maximum contributions are per employee. Please contact our office for the most up-to-date rates.

	State Unemployment Insurance	State Disability Insurance
Tax rate for a new employer	4.1%	—0—
Tax rate for employee	—0—	0.5%
Maximum wage amount per employee	$8,500	$95,585
Maximum employer amount per employee	$348.50	—0—
Maximum employee amount	—0—	$9,559

In addition to the above payroll taxes, you are required as an employer to withhold state personal income taxes (PIT) from each employee according to the number of exemptions claimed.

9. New York Payroll Tax Deposit Requirements

Due dates for combined deposits of SDI (state disability insurance) and SUI are based on an employer's **federal** payroll tax deposit schedule/requirement.

New York Quarterly Depositor. Quarterly tax payments are due and delinquent on the same dates as the Quarterly Wage and Withholding Report (NYS 45). (See monthly deposit requirements if you are a quarterly depositor but accumulate $700 or more in payroll withholding tax during one or more months of a quarter.) Although SUI and SDI are due quarterly, you may submit them with any SUI and SDI deposit.

Electronic Federal Tax Payment System (EFTPS) transactions for quarterly payments must settle into the state's bank account on or before the next business day following the last timely date for the quarter.

---

5 Great Marketing Questions

Q. What is the lifetime value of our customer?

Q. How often do our customers buy from us each year?

Q. What is the market potential?

Q. What do our customers really want?

Q. What does it cost us to acquire a new customer?

New York Monthly Depositor. You are required to make New York monthly SUI and PIT deposits if you are required to make federal monthly or quarterly deposits *and* you accumulate $700 or more in withholding during one or more months of a quarter. Monthly deposits are due by the fifteenth of the following month.

You will be required to make monthly SUI and SDI deposits if you are required to make federal next banking day or semiweekly deposits and, you accumulate $700 in *withholding* during one or more months of a quarter.

EFTPS transactions for monthly deposits must settle into the state's bank account on or before the next business day following the due date.

New York Semiweekly Depositor. You are required to make New York semiweekly SUI and SDI deposits if you are required to make federal semiweekly deposits *and* you accumulate more than $500 in *withholding* during one or more payroll periods. (If you accumulate $350-$500 in *withholding* during one or more pay periods, see monthly requirements below.) The semiweekly deposit schedule requires that if payday is Wednesday, Thursday, or Friday, then deposit is due by the following Wednesday, and if payday is Saturday, Sunday, Monday, or Tuesday, then deposit is due by the following Friday.

Semiweekly depositors always have three business days after the end of the semiweekly period to make a deposit. If any of the three weekdays after the end of a semiweekly period is a legal holiday, you will have one additional business day to make your deposit.

EFT transactions for semiweekly deposits must settle into the state's bank account on or before the next business day following the due date.

New York Next Banking Day Depositor. You are required to make New York next banking day SUI and SDI deposits if you are required to make federal next banking day deposits *and* you accumulate more than $500* in *withholding* during one or more payroll periods. (If you accumulate $350-$500 in PIT during one or more pay periods, see monthly requirements below.)

You may also want to review the New York Department of Labor website at www.labor.ny.gov

10. Employee vs. Independent Contractor

A major area of uncertainty and potential dispute relates to whether a worker is classified as an employee or as an independent contractor. All else being equal, it is much less costly to the employer if a worker is an independent contractor—avoiding Social Security and other payroll taxes. However, if someone is subsequently reclassified by the authorities as an employee, the penalties can be substantial. This can happen, for example, when a terminated "independent contractor" files for unemployment benefits and claims to have really been an employee.

The IRS has developed a twenty-factor control test to help determine whether the person providing the service should be classified as an employee or as an independent contractor

20 Factors

The key question to ask: "Do you 'control' the employee?" In other words, "Do you tell your employee when, where, and how to work?" If yes, then he or she is an employee.

ELEMENTS	EMPLOYEE	INDEPENDENT CONTRACTOR
1. Instructions	Employee is required to comply with instructions about when and where work is done.	An independent contractor decides how to do the job, establishes his/her own procedures, and is not supervised.
2. Training	Employee may be trained by other experienced employee working with him or her, by correspondence, by required attendance, or by other methods.	An independent contractor uses his/her own methods and receives no training from the principal.

ELEMENTS	EMPLOYEE	INDEPENDENT CONTRACTOR
3. Integration	If the worker's services are so integrated into an employer's operations that the success or continuation of the business depends on the performance of the services, it generally indicates employment.	An individual's performance of service and those of assistants affect his or her own business reputation.
4. Services rendered personally	If the services must be rendered personally, it indicates the employer is interested in the methods as well as results.	A contractor having the right to substitute another's services without the principal's knowledge suggests the existence of an independent relationship.
5. Hiring, supervising, paying assistants	If a worker hires or supervises an assistant at the employer's direction, he/she is acting as a representative of the employer.	An independent contractor hires, supervises, and pays assistants under a contract with him/her.
6. Continuing relationship	The existence of a continuing relationship between a worker and the person for whom he/she performs services indicates an employee status.	The relationship between an independent contractor and his/her client ends when the job is finished.
7. Set hours of work	Employer sets hours of work for the worker.	An independent contractor is the master of his/her own time.
8. Full-time work	Full-time work for the business is indicative of control by employer. Full time does not necessarily mean an eight-hour day or five-day week but may vary with the intent of the parties and nature of occupation.	An independent contractor is free to work whenever he/she chooses.
9. Work done on premises	An employee works on the employer's premises or on the location designated by employer.	An independent contractor can work away from the principal's premises.

ELEMENTS	EMPLOYEE	INDEPENDENT CONTRACTOR
10. Order or sequence of work	An employee performs services in order or sequence set by employer.	An independent contractor is free to perform services to complete the work as he/she prefers.
11. Reports	A submission of regular oral or written reports indicates control, since the worker must account for his/her actions.	An independent contractor is not required to file the reports that constitute a review of his/her work.
12. Payments by hour, week, month	Payment by hour, week, month indicates employee status.	Payment to contractors is usually by a flat fee for the job or by working hours.
13. Payment for worker's business and traveling expenses	Payment by employer indicates control over worker.	Are paid on a job basis, and the contractor takes care of all incidental expenses.
14. Tools and materials	Tools and materials are normally furnished by employer.	An independent contractor furnishes his/her own tools and materials.
15. The extent of the worker's investment	All necessary facilities are furnished by employer.	An independent contractor often (but not necessarily) has a significant investment status in the facilities he/she uses in performing services.
16. Profit and loss	When workers are insulated from loss or restricted in the amount of profit gained, they are usually employees.	The possibility of a profit or loss for the worker as a result of his/her services shows independent contractor status, who invests significant amounts of time or capital in his/her work without any guarantee of success.
17. Works for more than one person or firm	A worker may work for a number of people or firms and still be an employee of one or all of them because he/she works under control of each firm.	An independent contractor works for a number of persons or firms at the same time. He/she can work freely, not controlled by any firms.

ELEMENTS	EMPLOYEE	INDEPENDENT CONTRACTOR
18. Offers services to the general public	If a worker performs services alone, does not advertise his/her services to general public, does not hold licenses or hire assistants, and performs services on a continuing basis, it is an indication of an employment relationship.	An independent contractor is free to seek out business opportunities, advertise, maintain a visible business location, and is available in the general public.
19. Right to discharge	If the employer has the right to discharge a worker at will and without liability, the worker is considered an employee.	An independent contractor cannot be discharged as long as he/she produces a result that measures up to his/her contract specification; relationship can be terminated with liability.
20. Right to quit	The right to quit at any time without incurring liability indicates an employer-employee relationship.	If an individual agrees to complete a specific job and he/she is responsible for its satisfactory completion, it indicates the independent contractor status.

For more information, refer to IRS publication 15-A, Employer's Supplemental Tax Guide, and talk with us.

11. New York Independent Contractor

The Department of Labor (DOL) has four additional items to help determine whether the person providing the service should be classified as an employee or as an independent contractor.

ELEMENTS	EMPLOYEE	INDEPENDENT CONTRACTOR
21. Custom in industry and location	If the work is traditionally done by civil service employees under the direction of a supervisor, it is an indication of employment.	If the work is done by outside specialists, it is an indication of independence.

ELEMENTS	EMPLOYEE	INDEPENDENT CONTRACTOR
22. Required level of skill	A low level of technical skill is strong evidence of employment, since as the skill level declines, there is less room to exercise the discretion necessary for independence.	A high level of technical skill is important when combined with other factors such as owning a separate and distinct business.
23. Belief of the parties	It is an indication of employment if: Both parties (the worker and the state) believe the relationship is employment. Either party believes that the relationship is employment.	If the parties agree that the relationship is one of independence, it may be. However, consideration should be given to the fact that many individuals do not know how employment determinations are made and believe they are independent contractors because they are told they are.
24. Business decisions	Employees cannot make business decisions that would enable them to earn a profit or incur a financial loss.	Independent contractors make business decisions that enable them to earn a profit or incur a loss. Investment of the worker's time is not sufficient to show a risk of loss.

Report of Independent Contractor(s)

Any business or government entity that is required to file a federal Form 1099-MISC for services received from an independent contractor is required to retain Form W-9 filled by the independent contractor. Most often, Form W-9 is sent to independent contractors, consultants, and other self-employed workers. Form W-9 is also used by banks and other financial institutions to request tax information from customers.

Filling out a W-9 is pretty straightforward. Just provide your name and Social Security number, or the name and Employer Identification Number of your business.

By submitting a W-9, you are certifying that the tax ID number you are providing is correct and accurate. You also need to certify whether or not you are subject to withholding. Most taxpayers are exempt from backup withholding. The IRS might require backup withholding, however, if your name and tax identification number that you provide on the W-9 don't match with the IRS records or if you owe outstanding federal taxes, and the IRS has notified you.

The independent contractor reporting requirements apply if you hire an independent contractor and the following statements all apply:

- You are required to file a Form 1099-MISC for the services performed by the independent contractor.
- You pay the independent contractor $600 or more **or** enter into a contract for $600 or more.
- The independent contractor is an individual or sole proprietorship.
- You are advised to have an independent contractor's agreement signed by both parties (see sample).

12. Form 1099 Filing Requirements for Independent Contractors

Federal and New York rules have annual reporting requirements for payments to independent contractors. Payments are reported on form 1099 MISC. In general, you are required to file a form 1099 if you have paid a person at least $600 in rents or services (including parts and materials). You must have the name and address and SSN or FEIN for each payee. You can obtain this information during the year by requiring the person to complete a form W-9 when you engage them for their services.

It is extremely important to report the 1099 payment information correctly. The government agencies use this information to determine if the payee has included the income on his or her tax return.

You may want to review the instructions for Form 1099 at irs.gov. There are several exceptions to filing Form 1099.

How we can help

Please call us, and we will be pleased to help get you set up for payroll and payroll taxes and various reporting requirements.

Independent Contractor Agreement—Sample

Agreement is made this _____ day of _____, 20_
The following outlines our agreement:
You have been retained by _____
_____ as an independent contractor for the project of ____
_____.

You will be responsible for successfully completing the project according to specifications. The project is part time/ temporary and shall be completed by _____. (Date). Failure to meet this date will result in a reduction of payment. You will be responsible to carry whatever insurances, including workmen's compensation, and it is assumed that you carry adequate licenses to complete the job. If you do not carry insurance required by law, then we shall deduct a portion of your wages to pay for the insurance, or we have the right to let you go from the job.
You will be paid a fee of $_____.You will invoice us for your services rendered at the end of each month.
Payment will be made when invoice is received.

You:
  ♦ Will not be treated as an employee for federal or state income tax purposes
  ♦ Will not receive a regular salary but instead will be compensated directly related to services rendered
  ♦ Will be responsible for paying his/her own Social Security and Medicare taxes
  ♦ Won't be covered under the State Unemployment Insurance
  ♦ Won't receive employee benefits that are offered to regular employees
  ♦ Won't be covered by workers' compensation
  ♦ Won't be under the control of the employer as to how a job is done
  ♦ Will be issued a Form 1099 stating the earnings for the calendar year, if it is over $ 600.00

During the project you may be in contact with or directly working with proprietary information that is important to our company and its competitive position. All information must be treated with strict confidence and may not be used at any time or in any manner in work you may do with others in our industry.

The company reserves the right to cancel the contract for any reason. Payment for cancellation of the project shall be agreed upon.

The contractor will provide all equipment and supplies needed for this assignment and will pay for them at his own expense.

The contractor agrees that he will abide by all applicable labor laws, including paying for any employees he may use on the project in accordance with state and federal labor standards.

The contractor agrees to indemnify and hold harmless _____ (company) for any violations of state, federal law that may occur during the execution of the contract.

Agreed:
Independent Contractor_____ (Name)
_____ (sign)
Company Owner/Rep_____ (Name)
_____ sign)
Date: _____
This contract expires end of _____, 20__ unless specifically renewed.

Chapter 6
INCOME TAXES

*In this world nothing can be said to be
certain, except death and taxes.*
Benjamin Franklin

CHAPTER **6**

Income Taxes

Income tax laws are extensive, complicated, and constantly changing. While this chapter is not intended to cover all ramifications of income taxes, it does provide some general guidelines for complying with the main income tax rules.

1. Income Tax Reporting

Each type of legal entity is required to file a different type of income tax form, as follows:

a. **Sole Proprietorship:** A sole proprietorship is considered a component of the individual's personal tax return. Schedule C, the required tax form, is included with the owner's Form 1040. There is no special form for New York. If the business has net taxable income, then Schedule SE must be prepared to determine the amount of self-employment tax that is due to the federal government (this is the self-employed equivalent of Social Security taxes).

b. **Partnership:** A partnership is not a taxable entity. It is treated as a conduit through which taxable income is passed to the individual partners for inclusion in their respective tax returns. The partnership is required to file Federal Form 1065. For New York, a Form IT-204 is required. For New York City, Form NYC-204 is used. No income

> **Successful Business Owners**
>
> ✓ Work smarter *not* harder
> ✓ Measure accurately how they're doing
> ✓ Forecast ahead and monitor progress
> ✓ Control costs with budgets
> ✓ Have a financial strategy

tax is due with these forms; however, included with the forms is a Schedule K-1, which lists the various items of income and credits to be included on the individual partners' returns.

c. **C Corporation:** A C corporation is considered a taxable entity and is required to file a Federal Form 1120 and New York Form CT-4 and CT-3M/4M. New York City corporations should also file FORM 3L.

d. **S Corporation:** An S corporation is a type of corporation that has special treatment under the tax laws. Generally, this type of entity is treated in the same manner as a partnership, with certain exceptions. Tax forms required are Federal Form 1120S and New York Form CT-4S. New York City corporations should also file Form 3L.

e. **Limited Liability Company:** A limited liability company and its cousin, a limited liability partnership (used typically by professional service providers) are generally not taxable entities and are treated as a conduit though which taxable income is passed to the individual partners or members for inclusion in their respective tax returns. These entities are generally required to file the same forms as a partnership. No income tax is due with the forms; however, included with the forms is a Schedule K-1, which lists the various items of income and credits to be included on the returns of the individual partners or members.

However, if the company needs to change its filing entity, it has to file Form 8832—Entity Classification Election.

2. Estimated Tax Payments

In addition to the regular tax forms, the law specifies that if an estimate of the tax is not properly prepaid on a quarterly basis, a nondeductible underpayment penalty is to be levied. Since an estimate is based on forecasting the future, and liable to human error, the tax laws provide two safe-harbors to avoid the penalty for underpayment. If your payments for each quarter equal the lesser of 100 percent of the prior year's tax or 90 percent of the current year's tax, then the penalty can be avoided. In some cases you may have to pay 110 percent of the prior year federal tax liability to avoid the penalty. New York requires a minimum corporate estimate of $800, even if no tax is owed.

There are exceptions to the underpayment penalty, one of which is the annualized income installment method. Required quarterly payments can be calculated based on actual income and deductions in each quarter. If income was higher in later quarters of the year, this method may reduce the penalty by lowering required quarterly payments at the beginning of the year.

Estimates are filed using the following forms:

Corporate: Federal tax deposit Form 8109, deposited
with your bank.
New York Form IT 2669

Individual: Federal Form 1040-ES
New York Form IT 2105

3. Due Dates

Due dates of the various forms are:

a. Sole Proprietorship: Federal Form 1040 and New York Form IT 201 are due on April 15. Estimated tax payment forms (Federal Form 1040-ES and New York Form IT-2105) are due quarterly on

	April 15, June 15, September 15 and January 15.
b. *Partnership:*	Federal Form 1065 and New York Form IT 204 are due the fifteenth day of the fourth month after the end of the tax year—April 15 for almost all partnerships.
c. *C Corporation:*	Federal Form 1120 and New York Form CT-4 are due the fifteenth day of the third month after the end of the tax year. Federal tax deposit Form 8109 and New York Form IT 2668 are due the fifteenth day of the fourth, sixth, ninth and twelfth month of the tax year.
d. *S Corporation:*	Federal Form 1120S and New York Form CT-4S are due the fifteenth day of the third month after the end of the tax year. Federal tax deposit Form 8109 and New York Form Ct-400 are due the fifteenth day of the fourth, sixth, ninth and twelfth months of the tax year.
e. *Limited Liability Company:*	An LLC may be treated as a partnership or corporation for tax purposes. The due dates will follow the classification above.

4. Extensions

Businesses and individuals may request an extension of time to file tax returns. However, these extensions do not extend the time for paying the tax.

5. First Tax Return

The first tax return of a business is very important. Elections are made that will dictate the way the business is taxed for many years to come.

Some of the more significant elections that will need consideration are outlined below:

a. Election to capitalize and amortize costs incurred to organize the business. These can be legal, accounting, or similar fees paid to commence operations. Such costs are not normally considered expenses of the corporation and are not deductible unless this election is made.
b. Election to accrue vacation pay earned but not taken by employees at the end of the tax year. Without this election, vacation pay is not deductible until the year it is taken.
c. Accounting method used to report for tax purposes:
    - Cash
    - Accrual
    - Other hybrid method

d. Method of inventory valuation.
e. Method of accounting for long-term contracts.

The elections discussed above are only a few of those that may need to be considered in an initial return. It is important to plan how best to utilize elections to take advantage of some of the following provisions of the Federal and New York tax laws:

- Net operating loss carryovers
- Research and development tax credits
- Business energy tax credits
- New York tax credits

6. State Taxes

If your company conducts, or plans to conduct, business in more than one state, it is essential that you familiarize yourself with the applicable tax laws and filing requirements. If you are not in compliance, you may be prohibited from doing business in those states. You may also subject yourself to significant penalties and interest.

How we can help

Taxes are our "bread and butter"—the laws are very complicated, so we recommend that you retain us to prepare your income tax returns. Any amount you might save by doing your own returns can be more than offset by the costs of making mistakes.

But a bigger issue than making mistakes is missing the significant tax savings opportunities available to businesses, particularly on an initial return.

Proper tax planning is also essential to realize the greatest benefit from the income tax laws. This is a year-round process requiring communication on both sides—you and us. Please let us help you in this important area.

Chapter 7
ACCOUNTING AND BOOKKEEPING

You have to know accounting. It's the language of practical business life. It was a very useful thing to deliver to civilization. I've heard it came to civilization through Venice, which, of course, was once the great commercial power in the Mediterranean. However, double entry bookkeeping was a hell of an invention.
Charlie Munger
Vice Chairman Berkshire-Hathaway

CHAPTER 7
Accounting and Bookkeeping

As an owner of a business, it is vitally important that you have the financial information you need to run the business effectively. You will also need financial information to provide to outsiders such as the bank and to the taxing authorities.

The necessity for good, well-organized financial records cannot be overemphasized. One of the mistakes made by some entrepreneurs is not keeping good financial records and, therefore, not having sufficient information to make good business decisions or not receiving warning signals of potential problems such as a likely future cash crunch.

Good, timely financial reports do not necessarily require complicated bookkeeping or accounting systems. An appropriate system is like any tool used in your business; it needs to be sophisticated enough to provide the information you need but simple enough that you or your assistant or bookkeeper can run it.

Questions you will want to ask in developing your accounting and financial reporting system are:

1. Who will need and want to see the financial information?
2. What information do we need to manage the business?
3. What information will be needed to satisfy the government, regulatory, and taxing authorities?

Please seek our assistance in developing a system that will consistently provide the right information on a timely basis.

1. The Accounting Process

Accounting is the process of collecting, organizing, maintaining, and reporting financial information. Let's review the process:

Everything starts with the creation of source documents, which record your business transactions. Source documents include:

- Sales invoices
- Cash receipts
- Cash register tapes
- Purchase invoices
- Checks
- Miscellaneous, such as petty cash items

> **5 Key Performance Indicators (KPIs) for Every Business**
>
> ✓ Revenue
> ✓ Gross Profit %
> ✓ Accounts Receivable Days
> ✓ Average Transaction Value
> ✓ Overhead as a % of Revenue

Journals. Journals (also known as "books of original entry") are where the information from the source documents is recorded in a prescribed way.

- Sales are recorded in a sales journal
- Purchases are recorded in a purchase journal
- Cash receipts are recorded in a cash receipts journal
- Checks are recorded in a cash disbursements journal

General Ledger. Once all the source documents have been recorded in the journals, the summary totals are transferred to a general ledger, where the balances of each account are displayed. A listing of these account balances is known as a "trial balance."

What we have described to this point is generally referred to as "bookkeeping" or "write-up work". At the end of a time period—usually a month—we want to summarize everything that has been done during the period and create reports, known as "financial statements."

Adjusting Entries. But before we can generate the financial statements, we need to carefully review what's been done and make sure that "what the books say" reflects reality. Part of this activity involves reconciliations of the bank accounts, receivables, and payables.

We then make various adjusting entries to record such items as

- depreciation,
- payroll taxes,
- bad debts, and
- bank charges.

The next step is to prepare financial statements.

2. Financial Statements

A basic set of financial statements consists of a balance sheet, a profit and loss statement, and a statement of cash flow.

Balance Sheet. Your balance sheet reports the financial position of your company as of a given date. Think of it as a "snapshot" of the business. Your balance sheet has three elements: assets, liabilities, and equity. Assets are things you own. Examples include:

- Cash
- Accounts receivable
- Inventory
- Equipment
- Furniture and fixtures
- Deposits (such as rent deposits)

Liabilities are what you owe. Examples include:

- Accounts payable
- Notes payable
- Payroll taxes payable
- Accrued interest payable

Equity is the difference between what you own and what you owe (i.e., what's your worth). The equity section of the balance sheet is in turn broken down into subsections tracking how much the owner(s) contributed to the business, how much the business has made (or lost), and how much the owner(s) took out.

Profit and Loss Statement. Your profit and loss statement (also called an "income statement" but most frequently referred to as a P&L) shows the profit or loss of the business during a specific period of time. The elements of a P&L are:

- Income (or revenue)
- Cost of goods sold
- Operating expenses
- Net profit (or net income)

Operating expenses are usually grouped into categories, for example, as follows:

- Labor and personnel
- Marketing expenses
- Occupancy expenses
- Office expenses
- General and administrative
- Other

Design your own groupings to give yourself the information *you* need to run the business.

Cash Flow Statement. Your cash flow statement shows you the changes in your cash position over a period of time—where it came from and where it went. The cash flow statement is broken down into three major categories:

1. *Cash Flows from Operating Activities*—This represents the cash flow generated from the business, which will be different from the net profit because of changes in receivables, inventory, accounts payable, and fixed assets. (For example, buying inventory does not affect your P&L until you sell it, but it does affect cash.)
2. *Cash Flows From Investing Activities*—This represents the cash flow movement from buying or selling assets held for investment and similar activity.
3. *Cash Flows From Financing Activities*—This represents the cash flow movement from borrowing or repaying money and receiving or paying back money put in by the owner(s).

The cash flow statement helps you reconcile the age-old dilemma, "if we made all this money, why don't we have any cash?"

3. Responsibility for Bookkeeping and Accounting

Bookkeeping and accounting are such important functions that it makes sense early on to assign clear responsibilities for their regular, consistent execution.

Important questions for you to ask are:

1. Who will keep the books of the business?
2. Will your receptionist or assistant double as a part-time bookkeeper?
3. Will you have an outside bookkeeper that comes in periodically, or will the volume of activity require a full-time bookkeeper?

Business owners often decide to keep the books themselves, and underestimate the time commitment required. Other demands of the business (such as making sales!) may create a time crunch, resulting in record keeping receiving a low priority. Keeping the books requires regular allocation of time. Close control can be achieved by personally signing checks and scrutinizing key documents and records, such as the monthly bank statement.

Control Tip: Have all bank statements sent to your home address, so that you can perform a quick review before passing them to someone else to reconcile.

Let's revisit the steps in the bookkeeping and accounting process:

Source Documents. These are prepared by the business as part of normal day-to-day operations.

Journals. These are usually prepared in-house using an automated accounting program such as QuickBooks.

General Ledger. The general ledger is generally created as a by-product of the above steps when using a program such as QuickBooks.

Trial Balance. This is in effect a printout of the general ledger.

Adjusting Entries. Some of the adjusting entries can be made in-house, particularly on interim month-end closings. At year-end, we, as your CPAs, would make needed year-end adjusting entries.

Financial Statements. Interim financial statements can be prepared in-house depending on the level of expertise available. Year-end financial statements would normally be part of our responsibility or a coordinated effort.

As CPAs, we are available to assist in the bookkeeping and accounting function, depending on your needs and availability of time and personnel. For example, if you only want to produce the source documents, we can complete all the other steps. At the other end of the spectrum, you may be able to complete all the steps and just have us help with finalizing the year-end financial statements and tax returns.

4. Cash or Accrual Accounting

One of the decisions to be made early on is whether to keep your books on a cash or accrual basis.

The cash basis of accounting has the advantage of simplicity. Income is recorded when money is received, and expenses are recorded when money is paid out.

The **accrual basis** is a much better reflection of what is actually happening in your business. It matches the revenue generated in a particular time period with the costs and expenses of generating that revenue, even if the related cash receipts or disbursements take place in some other time periods. Income is recorded when you earn it (e.g., make a sale) and expenses are recorded when you incur them. Keeping books on an accrual basis is more time-consuming, but the information generated is worth the effort.

Whether you use the cash or accrual basis, it is often possible to report for tax purposes on a different, more advantageous basis. We can advise you on possibilities in your particular circumstances.

5. Internal Control

Internal control is a system of checks and balances designed to ensure that company assets are properly safeguarded and that the financial information produced is accurate and reliable. If you are personally handling all of the company's financial transactions, maintaining good internal control is relatively straightforward.

However, when a company grows to the size that delegating some functions becomes necessary, it is more difficult to ensure that all transactions are being accounted for properly. As soon as you delegate tasks and functions, potential internal control issues arise.

No matter the size of your business, you want to be able to answer yes to the following questions:

1. When we provide goods or services to our customers, can we be certain that sales are always properly recorded and the cash is collected?
2. When we pay out cash, can we be certain that we received the proper goods or services?

There are a number of steps to establishing good internal controls, the principal one being: do not let anyone control a financial function from start to finish. That way, for fraud to take place, you would have to have collusion.
Examples of internal control steps:

- The individual preparing sales invoices should be different from the person recording them.
- The person preparing and recording checks should not be allowed to sign them. And it's a good idea to require dual signatures on checks if it's practical.
- The person receiving the bank statement should not be the same person who reconciles the bank. As suggested already, have bank statements sent to your home address.

Sample Fraud Checklist
Fraud is a potential threat to every company. Review the checklist below, and if you answered no to any questions, an internal controls review might be a worthwhile exercise.

	Yes	No

1. Do you have a code of conduct that explicitly prohibits employees from committing fraud, having conflicts of interest, or engaging in any other form of illegal or unethical behavior?
   a. Have all your employees, vendors, and customers received a copy of it?
   b. Have key employees provided annual confirmation of their compliance?		

2. Do you have a clear company policy on time and expense reporting?		
3. Do you verify the credentials (including bank details) of all new vendors before they are authorized to supply your company?		
4. Do you make sure all disbursements are properly approved?		
5. Do you use direct deposit for payroll?		
6. Do you require two signatures on checks over a certain amount?		
7. Do you review the bank statements before anyone else does? You might want to consider having them sent to your home address.		
8. Do you review canceled checks (or copies) and match payee names with endorsements?		
9. Do you review invoices for any payees you don't recognize?		
10. Do you make sure that bank statements are reconciled each month and that your CPA reviews the bookkeeper's work periodically?		
11. Do you make sure everyone takes their full allotted vacation time?		
12. If something seems odd, whether it is a disbursement to an unfamiliar vendor or an unexpected expense, do you have a system in place to verify the information?		

SAMPLE ONLY—THIS CHECKLIST IS GENERAL BUSINESS ADVICE AND SHOULD NOT BE CONSTRUED AS SPECIFIC TO YOUR SITUATION. PLEASE CONSULT THE APPROPRIATE ADVISERS.

6. Computer Systems

Since the development of double-entry bookkeeping (first documented by an Italian monk, Luca Pacioli, in 1495), the advent of the computer has had the single greatest impact on accounting.

Virtually every business in America has a computer system of some kind, generally running some kind of accounting package. Several packages are available, and they are quite affordable, robust, and easy to learn. The most popular is QuickBooks, but there are several others. We have experience with a variety of accounting software packages that can help you run your business more efficiently. It is important to choose software that will best meet your particular needs.

How we can help

We are available to assist you with the following:
- Setting up a proper accounting system
- Helping you identify your key performance indicators (KPIs) and develop a measuring and monitoring system
- Establishing appropriate internal controls
- Selecting a computerized accounting package, setting up the system, and providing training

---

CHAPTER 8
CASH MANAGEMENT

Profit in business comes from repeat customers, customers that boast about your project or service, and that bring friends with them.
W. Edwards Deming

CHAPTER 8
Cash Management

Cash is king! The lifeblood of any business is its ability to collect cash. We often encounter small businesses that are profitable yet don't generate enough free cash to pay the day-to-day expenses and the owners.

Being able to anticipate cash resources is an important part of running a successful enterprise.

1. Starting the Analysis

The starting point for forecasting your cash flow is the volume of sales you expect to generate. Your sales forecast must be as finely tuned as possible.

Some factors to consider in your sales forecast include:

- Expected market share
- Sales history
- Competitive analysis
- Product lines
- Number and quality of sales people or distributors
- Seasonality
- Local economic conditions
- Time horizon

2. Cash Collections

Once you have completed your sales forecast, you now need to calculate how sales will convert to cash. So you will need to estimate:

- What percentage of sales are paid in cash?
- What percentage are credit sales, where you have to carry accounts receivable?

- What percentage are credit card sales, where processing fees will be deducted?
- What percentage of the credit sales do you expect to collect in:
  o thirty days?
  o ninety days?
  o More than ninety days?
- What percentage might we never collect (bad debts)?

> **Successful Business Owners**
>
> ✓ Systemize the business to help people work more effectively
> ✓ Have written procedures to help employees follow the system
> ✓ Have a clear organizational chart with clear reporting guidelines
> ✓ Have job descriptions for all roles in the company

- What discounts are you planning to offer for prompt payment?
- How much of our collections are for sales tax, which will need to be remitted to the taxing authority?
- What other sources of cash are planned (such as rents from subtenants, loans, or owner investment)?

Once you are comfortable with the timing of the collections of funds from sales and other sources, it's time to look at the costs, expenses, and other cash outflows of your business.

3. Cash Outflows

As you start to work on the outflow or disbursement side of your forecast, you will want to consider the following questions related to cost of sales:

- If your business requires inventory, do you purchase the merchandise from others, or do you purchase component parts and assemble them?
- What are the credit terms your vendors are willing to offer? Do you have to pay for purchases on a COD

basis, or can you get credit for thirty, forty-five, or even sixty days?
- What costs are required to convert purchased items into salable merchandise?
- What supplies are needed to be kept on hand to pack and ship merchandise?
- How many employees will you need and at what cost?
- How much machinery will be required and at what cost?

Once you have addressed the cost of sales issues, including the costs of carrying inventory and processing it, it's time to consider all the other expenses of operating the business.

If we take all the ongoing monthly expenses as a given, let's look at some other expenditures that you may face in the first year of business. Here's a partial checklist:

- First and last month's rent
- Rent security deposit
- Purchase of furniture, or deposit if a rental
- Purchase of fixtures and equipment
- Purchase of computers, peripherals, and installation costs
- Utility deposits
- Organization costs (if you're a corporation)
- Lawyer's fees for drafting agreements, incorporating your business, and reviewing your lease agreement
- Accountant's fees for setting up the accounting system and establishing the chart of accounts
- Tenant improvements
- Business licenses
- Stationery
- Signs
- Logo design fees
- Initial inventory of supplies
- Loan repayments

When you're preparing your forecast, it may seem as if the list of costs and expenses is endless. However, it is imperative to make the list as detailed as possible to ensure that you have sufficient funds to make your operation viable and to avoid running out of cash. Remember, one of the primary causes of small business failure is undercapitalization

In addition to determining cash outlays you will have to make, it is critical to determine the timing of such payments. A good rule of thumb for cash flow planning is to assume that you are going to have to pay your expenses sooner than you think and that you will collect your cash slower than you anticipate. If you use this approach, any negative surprises should be minimal.

Preparing cash flow projections can be time consuming and tedious. We can help! We have software programs that can do most of the "heavy lifting" and where you can do "what if" analysis and get an immediate answer. Your personal involvement in the process is, of course, critical because these are your projections, *not* ours, and only you know what it takes to run the business.

The more effort **you** put into developing the cash flow projections, the more accurate and useful they will be. You may also discover potential savings that you had not previously considered.

How we can help

We are here to assist you with strategic planning, cash management, profit improvement, and benchmarking—these are all services designed to help your business reach its full potential.

CHAPTER 9
FINANCING YOUR BUSINESS

Sometimes when you innovate, you make mistakes. It is best to admit them quickly, and get on with improving your other innovations.
Steve Jobs

CHAPTER 9
Financing Your Business

Financing is the engine of commerce, and in this chapter we will address the issue of obtaining credit and financing your business. Most businesses will have to access financing at some point along the way.

You may need capital for the initial outlays prior to opening your business, or you may require funds for expansion or for additional working capital during seasonal peaks. Generally, business financing can take two forms: debt or equity.

Debt means borrowing money. Loans for start-up businesses usually come from one or more of these sources:

- Vendor or trade credit
- Personal credit cards
- Family
- Friends
- Banks
- Small Business Administration (SBA) guarantees
- Leasing companies
- Customers or clients
- Specialist lenders
- Investors

Equity involves giving up an ownership interest in exchange for money or other assets. This can take many forms, depending on which kind of legal entity you have selected.

If you have a partnership, you might sell a regular partnership interest. If you have a limited partnership (such as an LLC), you might sell a limited partnership interest.

If you have a corporation, you can issue common stock, preferred stock, stock options, or warrants, or a combination. This is a complex area and subject to very strict federal and state regulations designed to protect investors. Get you attorney involved *before* you start discussions with potential investors.

1. Financing Alternatives

As we have just outlined, a number of different types of debt and equity financing

> ## The Four Ways
> ## to Grow Your Business
>
> 1. Increase your prices.
> 2. Increase your number of customers and how often they do business with you.
> 3. Increase the amount your customers spend with you each transaction.
> 4. Decrease your expenses.

exist. Financing may even be a combination of debt *and* equity tailored to fit your company's requirements.

Let's look at the different sources of financing in more detail.

2. Debt Financing Sources

Vendor or Trade Credit. An important source of financing for small companies is credit from vendors and suppliers. Many suppliers will initially ask for cash on delivery (COD) or a prepayment before starting on your order. Most suppliers will offer you credit terms once you have gained their confidence by continuing to do business with them and paying on time. Establishing good relationships with vendors is essential, because if you buy on credit, you can often resell the purchased goods or services to your customers before you have to pay for them. In accounting parlance, this is called "lag the payable."

Many vendors will rely on your trade credit history as you establish additional vendor relationships. Trade credit terms vary depending on the type of purchase you make, the industry you are buying from, and the industry you are in. It makes sense to contact a number of vendors and even to pay a higher price for goods and services in exchange for more liberal payment terms.

Personal Credit Cards. An astonishing number of small businesses actually use personal credit cards as a major source of financing. In fact, prior to going into business, many people apply for new credit cards just to have some credit available to them. The downside, of course, is that credit cards often have a very high rate of interest, particularly after they pass the low-interest "tease" period. Also, having too many credit cards can negatively affect your credit rating. This should be the lender of last resort.

Family and Friends. Many businesses are launched with help from family and friends, who are more likely to be flexible on repayment terms. Written agreements are a "must." Business owners should not guarantee results and should be cautious of these arrangements, as they may lead to conflicts with their own friends and relatives.

Banks. Banks typically lend to small businesses on a secured basis using equipment, inventory, or accounts receivable. The more liquid and readily salable the assets you can offer as collateral, the more acceptable they are likely to be to a banker. Loans from a bank may take several forms, such as the following:

- A line of credit that allows you to borrow up to a predetermined maximum as you need it and pay it back as funds from operations become available
- A note payable in full on an agreed date
- An installment loan for the purchase of a specific asset, such as a computer or office furniture
- A longer-term fully amortized loan over three to five years

Unless you have a long-established credit history and a strong balance sheet, the bank will require personal guarantees from the principals.

Generally the banks look at the five Cs: capital, collateral, cash flow, character, and condition.

Small Business Administration (SBA) Guarantees. The SBA, an agency of the federal government, has a program whereby it will guarantee up to 90 percent of a loan to a small business. Most banks participate in this program. The SBA can also guarantee mortgages if you are buying your premises or guarantee leases if you are leasing. A good credit score, accurate business plan, and in some cases two years of business tax returns showing profits are also being asked.

Leasing Companies. In today's business environment, it is common to acquire equipment through a lease agreement. Leasing companies are willing to take a higher degree of risk than banks, and, accordingly, their funding is more expensive than commercial bank loans.

Leases typically run for three to five years with monthly lease payments—and then at the end of the lease, there is a payoff amount, either preagreed or fair market value, which allows you to get ownership of the asset. The effective interest rate is not stated in the lease agreement (since it's technically not a loan), but we can calculate it for you to make sure that leasing is the appropriate decision.

Businesses that are equipment heavy, such as baking, dentistry, restaurants, and orthopedic doctors are typical candidates for this type of financing.

The requirements are an excellent FICO score and a small down payment. One is advised to obtain services of an attorney for signing the contracts.

Customers or Clients. Often, the impetus for going into business is a favorite customer or client who says, "You should go out on your own," and who promises to do business with you. Asking for a modest loan is a good way to test their sincerity and finance your business. It also guarantees they are going to patronize the business! In accounting parlance, it is called "leading the receivable." Generally, companies that sell "hot products" or state of the art services can command this type of financing.

Specialist Lenders. Specialist lenders specialize in financing a particular type of acquisition (such as a medical practice) or a particular type of asset (such as a printing press).

Investors. Investors may structure all or part of their investment as a loan, as this will give them greater security. Such a loan will likely be convertible into equity, at the investor's option.

Accounts Receivable Financing. This is based upon the credit of your customers. Lending companies, also known as "factoring companies," get an ownership of your receivables.

The advantage is that you get financing right away. Garment and textile companies are ideal targets for this kind of financing.

PO—Purchase Order Financing This financing is based upon the gross margin of your business. Importers, wholesalers, and traders get into this form of financing. Banks and financial institutions use this kind of financing when they have confirmed orders from customers.

Merchant Cash Advances. Retailers such as restaurants with substantial credit card sales are a party to such financing. The financing is used for inventory purchases or expansion of the business. The owner can raise from $2,000 to $500,000.

The requirements are consistent monthly credit card volume and business history for at least three to six months. Profitability and credit score are not important criteria.

3. Equity Financing Sources

Equity financing means selling a portion of your business. You may have already decided to take in partners in exchange for an investment or you have family or friends who have invested in exchange for equity.

If these are not available or do not yield sufficient capital, there are professional investors to consider.

Venture capital companies. A venture capital company is in the business of taking risks. It is usually backed by a group of investors who may be individuals or corporations. The investors are represented by a management group that evaluates potential investments and manages the existing investments.

The cost of venture capital financing is high compared to other forms of financing, but that's because venture capitalists are dealing with high-risk situations that most lenders wouldn't contemplate, and there are usually no viable alternatives.

A venture capital firm will expect to get back at least three to seven times its investment over a five-year period. The venture capital firm can provide depth of experience and management assistance in areas where your management team may be weak. It can also provide valuable contacts and introductions. The cost of venture capital is measured in terms of the portion of your company you must give up in order to obtain the level of investment you need.

They may take up to 60 percent of the stake in your company's valuation. Financing is only obtained through milestone accomplishment. Owners may tend to lose "freedom" in their own start-up. This type of financing is responsible for only about 6 percent of the start-ups.

Private individuals. Sometimes successful individuals who have accumulated substantial wealth get into the business (or hobby) of investing in start-ups and other small companies. They are referred to as "business angels."

The business acumen and contacts of these individuals can be a valuable asset to your business. An individual investor can react to an opportunity more quickly than a venture capital firm and can be more flexible in the type of investment structure used.

There are different types of "angels" for different types of businesses. In 2012, $60B came from friends and families, and $20B can from real "angels."

4. Recent Concepts

ROBS—Rollover-as-business start-up. This is very complex transaction involving your retirement funds that are saved in your tax-deferred 401(k) or IRAs.

The savings in your retirement funds will own the stock of your company. In return, the owner can access the funds.

The advantage for the business owner is that though the owner has control over his funds and destiny, the associated risks are that the monies are invested only in one basket, and also compliance with the Internal Revenue Code is difficult.

Internet-Based Lending

P2P—Peer to Peer Loans. The individual lenders actually compete as in eBay manner to lend to small business owners.

The loans can be used for small-business funding and debt consolidation. Loans are in the range of $1,000 to $ 35,000. The transaction fees and the origination fees vary.

Crowd Funding. These finance start-ups. The owner can raise up to $1 million annually or $2 million if the audited statements are provided.

There are two basic kinds of proposals. The owner can give up equity in exchange for funds or provide service or products annually in exchange for funds.

The owner has to give a detailed business proposal. There is always a danger of the proposal being exposed to copycats.

5. How Do I Get the Money?

Regardless of the type of financing you're looking for, the process of obtaining it is the same. Develop a business plan that addresses these five basic questions:

1. What is your business proposition, and how will you make it successful?
2. Do you have the necessary experience, and have you done your homework?
3. How much money do you need?
4. How will you spend the money?
5. How will you pay it back?

The business plan usually covers a three-to five-year period and includes financial forecasts. Financial forecasts are like weather forecasts—the further out you go, the less reliable they become.

Here's a typical table of contents for a business plan:

1. Executive summary (including a statement of purpose and policy)
2. Background

3. Details of the product or service
4. Details of management and personnel
5. Details of other assets and resources
6. Marketing information
7. Financial information
8. Projected profit and loss statements
9. Time frames

How we can help

Because we have been in practice in this industry for a long time, we know most of the bankers and other funding sources. We are pleased to make introductions as appropriate.

We can also assist you in developing your business plan.

We can also help you to get upgrade your credit score to a very pristine one.

CHAPTER 10
INSURANCE

There is only one boss. The customer. And he can fire everybody in the company from the chairman on down, simply by spending his money somewhere else.
Sam Walton

CHAPTER **10**
Insurance

Insurance is not the favorite outlay for new businesses—one more place where money goes out and nothing comes in. That is, until something goes wrong. Then it's a great investment.

Many different insurance policies are available to businesses. Your accountant and insurance agent can help you review the amounts and kinds of coverage required to insure against both the general and specific risks that could have a significant impact on your business. The terms of your building or office lease or mortgage may require certain kinds of insurance coverage in specified minimum amounts. If you have leased equipment or have borrowed money from a bank or other lender, insurance requirements will likely be in those agreements.

Insurance companies typically offer package policies, which can be customized to provide comprehensive coverage of your unique needs. Make sure that your insurance policies are thoroughly reviewed each year—things change.

1. Policies

Here are some insurance policies that may be required or appropriate to your business:

1. ***Workers' Compensation Insurance***. Workers' compensation insurance coverage is mandatory in the state of New York. Employees are covered for on-the-job injuries and off-the-job injuries as well as vehicle coverage. Your insurance agent can explain the details of required coverage and rating systems, and can assist with policy purchase. Exemptions are allowed for owner/employees.

2. ***Health Insurance***. Health insurance is the principal benefit offered by employers and the most sought after by employees. Much has changed recently with the enactment of the Patient Protection and Affordable Care Act (also known as Obamacare), which is intended to provide a minimum level of coverage to most individuals. It requires most US citizens and legal residents to carry health insurance—some people will be eligible for tax credits to help pay for coverage, and those opting not to buy will be subject to penalties. The subject has become very complex, and it is impossible to cover the entire gamut in this book. You must, however, talk to your accident and health coverage insurer for more on this.

The new act does not require you as an employer to offer health insurance, but it does incentivize you in two ways:

- Each state will set up an "exchange" where small businesses can pool their risks, which presumably will save money.
- A Small Employer Health Insurance Tax Credit is available with a tax credit of up to 35 percent of an employer's contributions.

3. ***Property and Casualty Insurance***. This covers you against the loss of property by fire, theft, etc. Equipment should be insured for its replacement value.

If a new lathe costs $10,000, that is what it must be insured for. What the lathe is worth secondhand or what its recorded at on your books is irrelevant. If you lose your lathe, the proceeds will be needed to buy you a new one. The replacement value of equipment is often much higher than you think. Insurance on leased equipment will also generally be your responsibility.

4. ***Vehicle Insurance***. All vehicles have to be insured— at least for public liability.

Tip: To make sure you don't have a catastrophic loss of data in the event of loss or destruction of your computer systems, consider using an online backup service.

---

5. ***Product Liability***. This covers you in case any products that you manufacture or supply cause injury or damage to a third party or their property.

6. ***Professional Liability Insurance***. This type of insurance (also known as malpractice insurance) is common to professionals and is often mandated for certain professions, such as accounting and law to cover claims from clients for negligent acts, errors, or omissions. Other professionals, such as management consultants or IT consultants, are advised to investigate this type of coverage.

Key Credit Policy Questions

1. Are all new customers asked for suitable credit references?
2. Are credit references checked?
3. Are credit limits set, reviewed, and adhered to?
4. What is the system to handle delinquent receivables?

7. ***Life Insurance***. Your own life should be insured so that your family is protected from economic hardship in the event of your demise. The amount of coverage needed will depend on several factors, including the number of your dependents, their ages, or what other assets you have. Whole life insurance may be appropriate if you can afford it; otherwise, term insurance provides needed coverage at a modest cost.

8. ***Disability Insurance***. Make sure you consider disability insurance to protect against the possibility of a long-term disability or illness. A person in their forties is fifteen times more likely to be unable to work because of illness or disability than from death.

9. ***Key Person Insurance***. Key person insurance allows a business to insure the life or health of any employee whose death or prolonged absence would cause the business to suffer. It is ordinary life or health insurance, but with the business as the beneficiary.

10. ***Business Interruption***. Covers the loss of revenue should your business be forced to shut down due to reasons beyond your control, such as flood, fire, or earthquake.

11. ***Legal Fees***. Insurance is generally available to businesses to cover your legal fees should you be involved in a lawsuit.

12. ***Employee Fidelity Bond***. This covers the risk of loss from theft or dishonesty by employees. If your business deals in large amounts of cash, negotiable securities, or similar types of assets, you are well advised to consider this coverage. In fact, it is appropriate for any business where an employee has potential access to assets of the business, customers, or clients. Certain businesses are required to carry this type of insurance.

13. ***Umbrella Coverage.*** This covers losses over and above the limits of your other policies. Umbrella policies are especially valuable if you, or your business, have a net worth requiring protection in the event of a catastrophic loss.

14.***Buyout Insurance.*** Your business may have a requirement for the remaining shareholders or partners to buy out the interest of a shareholder or partner who dies. This can be covered by buyout insurance.

There are many other types of policies and reasons to consider them. Check with a qualified insurance broker who specializes in dealing with businesses.

When it comes to insurance, just follow this rule:

Do not take insurance that does not cover an event that results a financial loss such as a loss of breadwinner or a bad auto accident.

Rule of two Cs: Catastrophic loss and comprehensive coverage.

You are better off without the following insurances:
Credit life
Credit disability insurance
Mortgage life insurance
Dental insurance (big costs can be covered by a policy)
Car-loan gap insurance
Wedding insurance

Travel Insurance:

You may cover yourself for vacation protection. Please read the policy guidelines.

You can compare policies at Insuraemytrip.com or squaremouth.com.

When you are traveling, check your existing auto policy to see if it covers both medical and liability.

Insurance is like any other product you purchase. Do your homework. Before you buy, get lots of input about your needs and options.

How we can help

Call us, and we'll be pleased to recommend a qualified insurance broker.

CHAPTER 11

SELECTING PROFESSIONAL ADVISERS

You can't operate a company by fear, because the way to eliminate fear is to avoid criticism. And the way to avoid criticism is to do nothing.
Steve Ross

Chapter 11
Selecting Professional Advisers

Building a successful business involves developing alliances and a network of trusted advisers.

We're here to help. We will be pleased to provide services in the areas where we specialize.

These include:

- Income tax preparation
- Tax planning
- Accounting
- Bookkeeping
- Auditing
- Payroll and sales taxes
- Wealth management
- Financial planning
- Strategic planning
- Profit improvement
- Benchmarking
- Key performance indicator monitoring

> **Successful Business Owners**
>
> ✓ Listen to audiotapes of great minds
> ✓ Read management books
> ✓ Attend seminars of great speakers

We are also pleased to introduce you to other professionals:

- Attorneys
- Bankers
- Insurance brokers
- Real estate agents
- Printers
- IT consultants
- Payroll services
- Financial advisors
- Pension consultants

Please call us anytime—we're here to help.

We are always willing to spend an hour with someone starting a new business, *at no charge*!

When you start a business, you have to change your mind-set to having new "friends." You existing friends are more likely to tell you that you cannot make it.
Your three new friends should be the following:

1. Accountant/business coach
2. Banker
3. Financial planner

The more you spend time with them, the more you are likely to succeed.

How we can help

We can help you create a team from bankers to business coaches to financial planners.

CHAPTER 12

TRAITS OF A SUCCESSFUL BUSINESS OWNER

"The only way to do great work is to love what you do. If you haven't found it yet, keep looking. Don't settle."
Steve Jobs

CHAPTER 12
Traits of a Successful Business Owner

Over one million businesses are started every year in the United States as per the Department of Commerce. Eighty percent fail before a five-year period. Another 80 percent of the survivors fail during the next five years. The net result is that at the end of ten years only four out of one hundred businesses are still in existence! Staggering but true!

So what are the traits of a successful business owner?

1. You are a natural leader. The business owner defies convention and thinks differently. True leaders create clarity of direction, priorities, and expectations. He or she is a driving force in different functions of the business. A leader creates a team, motivates it, and gets results. Set a vision so that other could follow.
2. Hard work cannot be underemphasized. It goes without saying that a new business owner wears several hats; he or she is an entrepreneur/manager/marketer, etc. What is of utmost importance is, "What are you working hard on?"
3. Creativity is what distinguishes an employee and an employer.
4. Nothing can be accomplished if the owner is not in great shape.
5. If you are risk averse, then business is not meant for you. Risk taker means that you are very informed to make a calculated decision. Step out of the comfort-zone and take ongoing courage.
6. The attitude of a successful business owner is very determined, can face adversity, and is very insistent on being successful.

*The role your personal profile plays
in your business's success*

Are you a heart-dominant entrepreneur like Starbucks's Howard Schultz? Smarts dominant like Jeff Bezos of Amazon? Guts dominant like Virgin's Richard Branson? Or do you carry the luck trait like Tony Hsieh of Zappos? Four traits drive decision-making and, ultimately, success.

Your entrepreneurial profile impacts your business, from starting up, to scaling it, to shifting strategy, to selling it. At these turning points, it's important to know which traits you should dial up or dial down and what kind of people you may need beside you. "Having this degree of self-awareness may be the best marker of a successful entrepreneur—even more critical than having a high IQ," Tjan says.
Most entrepreneurs tend to overemphasize the formal business plan at inception. Seventy percent of those businesses that had a successful exit did not start with a formal business plan.

People matter more than ideas, and the general business model matters more than an overly detailed financial plan at the early stage—because those financial projections will never come out as planned, anyhow.

The Four Key Attributes of Successful Entrepreneurs:

Heart. A heart-dominant person kicks things off with passion and fire. He or she conjures up a great idea—a venture's seed or bulb and will simply believe that the right things will happen, and the bulb will grow.

Smarts. The smart-dominant individual is best suited to seeing patterns faster than anyone else and providing structure, analysis, and an actionable plan. He or she can be a highly successful business-builder.

Guts. Those with guts have the thick skin and fortitude to initiate and try something new, the guts to endure, and the guts to evolve. The guts trait can be divided up into risk takers and those who tolerate risk.

Luck. Most entrepreneurs benefit from luck at one time or another in their careers, even though luck appears to be chaotic and unpredictable. Those who seem to be "luckier" than others tend to be optimistic, intellectually curious, and humble.

By knowing what you are good at and where you have gaps, you are in a better position to identify people who will complement you to join the team. For example, if you are a heart-dominant entrepreneur, you are probably better served by a partner or a consultant who complements you with, say, a smarts-guts profile.

How we can help

We can review your business plan and make it bullet-proof.

Checklist to Start a Successful Business

Dear business owner:

Congratulations! You have now taken a giant step in opening your own business! The decisions you make today will have a significant impact on the future growth of your business. As an entrepreneur, you will control your destiny and create something of which you can be proud.

Every day, you will be responsible for making vital decisions affecting your business, employees, and customers. It's important to be educated before making these decisions and to hire qualified professionals to assist you in the process. Handling all of the variables pertaining to revenues, inventories, employees, competitors, pricing, and taxes can seem a daunting task at times.

With so many decisions to be made, many legal and financial decisions may be left unaddressed. These decisions might seem unimportant; however, it could make the difference between success and failure of your business.

This checklist explores some essential steps toward *protecting your assets, savings on taxes, and the road map to your wealth building.* As you start answering this checklist, you should be able to convert your unknowns to a path of more realistic solutions.

You are on a journey, and the journey itself is a success.

1. **Mission Statements:**
   (This is designed to say in a brief format what your company exists for. It should reflect a deeper sense of commitment and meaning than making money.)

+ What gets you up in the morning?
+ What do you live for?
+ What do you want out of life?
+ What do you consider the purpose of your life?
+ Did you make a mission statement in one sentence? (twenty-five words)

2. Vision Statements:

(This defines where you want to be as time passes and how you want to be remembered.)

+ What is the purpose of your life?
+ What do you want your future to be?
+ Can you write your own obituary/epitaph?

3. Personal Issues:

(Purpose of business is to meet the goals and needs of the family.)

+ Is your spouse in the business?
+ Are your children going to be part of the business? As employees or as shareholders?
+ Do you have retirement plans?
+ Are you planning to have an employee take over the business?
+ Do you have what it takes to be a businessperson?
  ❖ Leadership qualities and determination
  ❖ Physical stamina—physical fitness
  ❖ Are you capable of wearing many hats?

4. Business Plans:

(This is the detailed strategic game plan as to how to achieve the objectives. It is written and reviewed by a good accountant.)

+ Business plan in place?
+ Financial projections—one year, three years, five years?
+ Have you identified
  ❖ A sharp accountant?
  ❖ Generous banker? (Area in which we can help)
  ❖ Good lawyer?

- Do you have a board of directors?
- Do you have an analysis of competition, markets, etc.?
- Do you have a two-page executive summary?

5. **Corporate Set-Up:**
(Deciding on the right corporate structure is vital, as it has long-term implications in terms of taxes, IRS audits, personal liability, and benefits planning.)
- Do you have the right business structure? (LLC, C Corp., S Corp., or PCs)
- Is your company registered with the state?
- Do you have the corporate book with corporate seal, stock certificates, and transfer ledger?
- Do you have a Federal ID Number?
- If a corporation, did you file for subchapter S election?
- Did you select the correct year-end?
- Did you maintain a "minute book" to document all important decisions?

6. **Banking and Finance:**
(A good bank should offer interest-bearing savings account, overdraft account against the checking account, a corporate credit card, and Internet banking.)
- Opened checking account for issuance of checks.
- Opened savings account for depositing all revenues.
- Set up these two accounts such that there is automatic transfer when funds are needed.
- Do you have an overdraft account in case of an emergency?
- Order checks? Three checks on a page?
- Do you receive monthly bank statements on a calendar month basis?
- Do you have "seed capital" for initial investment?
- Do you have working capital till break-even point?
- Do you know about SBA (Small Business Administration) loans?

7. Licenses and Permits:

(These are mandatory to conduct business and should be obtained before the start of the business. These are normally displayed in your place of business.)

- License for the contractor, if any?
- Business license?
- Liquor/cigarette/lotto licenses?
- Any trademarks, patents, copyrights to be registered? (Intellectual property)

8. Minority Certification:

(Certification helps in doing business with the numerous state and city agencies. It increases revenue and levels the competitive playing field.)

- If you are a minority, you can obtain the following certifications:
  - ❖ Small Disadvantages Business (SDB) called the "8A program." (federal program)
  - ❖ Women Business Enterprise (WBE) State Program for women business owner
  - ❖ Small Disadvantages Business (SBE) State Program for small business under $20 million in gross revenue

(Certification helps in becoming a preferred vendor for city, state, and federal agencies.)

9. Buy-Sell Agreement/Valuation/Exit Strategy

(This helps in exiting your business in case of single ownership or selling your shares in case of multiple partners.)

- Do you have an operating document among partners?
- If you have more than two partners, you need to have a buy/sell agreement.
- Do you have an agreement that the business will be valued on December 31 of every year?
- Do you have an exit strategy for your business?

10.Sales:

(Revenue, the main objective of the business, has to be planned carefully.)
+ What is the revenue model?
+ Accept payments by cash, check, and credit card?
+ How do you record sales?
+ Credit terms? Discount terms?

11.Insurances:

(Some of the insurances are mandatory by law. Others are required as they protect you from lawsuits.)
+ If there is at least one employee (other than the owner) have you applied for disability insurance? [Disability is for off-the-job injuries.]
+ Have you applied for workmen's compensation? [Workmen's comp covers on-the-job injuries.]
+ Liability insurance covering product liability, business liability, etc.?
+ Umbrella insurance?
+ Health insurance for self and spouse?

12.Lease or Buy?

(This is an important decision from the owner's standpoint, having many tax and cash flow implications.)
+ Autos?
+ Machines?

13.Premises:

(A major decision point for any business both from the location and the cash flow standpoint.)
+ Renting or owning your place of business?
+ Do you have a long-term lease? If yes, is it a gross or net lease?
+ Do you have a home office? If yes, do you have a specified area?
+ Have you taken pictures of the home office and kept them in a separate file?

14. Labor Compliance and Policies:

(Familiarity with these laws assists the owner in managing the employees efficiently and effectively.)

+ Are you aware of the various labor compliance policies?
+ Do you have a copy of the summary for ready reference?
+ Are you aware of:
  ❖ OSHA (Occupational Safety and Health Administration)?
  ❖ Local laws covering signage, snow removal, garbage?
  ❖ American Disabilities Act?
  ❖ Immigration law regarding employment?
  ❖ Discrimination law poster requirements?
+ Is there a formal copy of the office policy?

15. Office Administration:

(These procedures need to be well organized for the effective running of the office.)

+ Stationery/envelopes printed
+ Business cards-printed
+ Invoices
+ Letterheads
+ Water/coffee
+ Garbage collection
+ Alarm system?
+ Refrigerator and microwaves

16. Assets and Automation:

(Technology planning is another area vital from communication and customer service standpoints.)

+ Computers—how many?
+ Printers/scanner/copier machine
+ Fax machines
+ Telephone system
+ Postage meter
+ E-mail address.
+ Telephone and fax numbers
+ Credit card machine

17. Inventory/Merchandise:

(Physical accounting of quantities and prices is important to make profits.)

- Have you identified your suppliers?
- Have you determined the cost and quantities?
- What are the payment terms? (cash/credit)
- Do you take physical inventory every month?
- Do you track usage of inventory?

18. Agreements:

(Well-written agreements ensure a harmonious functioning of the employees, sales personnel, and shareholders.)

- Is the rental agreement in place?
- Are there any lease agreements for machines?
- Car lease agreement?
- Key employee agreement?
- Sales personnel agreement?
- Agreements with independent contractors, consultants?
- Shareholders or partners agreements?

19. Payroll:

(There are legal and tax requirements for disbursements of compensation to hired personnel.)

- Do you have proper documentation for every employee?
- Do you know to differentiate between an employee and an independent contractor?
- Do you have resumes and noncompete agreements?
- Do you check the references of your employees?
- Do you have a W-4 and I-9 for every W-2 employee? (copy of Social Security card and driver's license)
- Do you have W-9 and independent contractor's agreement for 1099 employee?
- Do you have a policy or a manual for employees? (Health insurance, timings)
- Are you filing quarterly payroll tax returns—both federal and state on time?

* Do you maintain proper wage and hour records?

20. Sales Tax:

(These are called "trustee" taxes and are the fiduciary responsibility of the owner.)

* Are you liable for sales tax?
* Are you familiar with sales tax filing?
* Do you collect sales tax from customers?
* Do you have a sales tax registration number?

21. Accounting and Taxes:

(Analyzing your operations is crucial for the continuity of profitable operations.)

* Is your bookkeeping handled by a responsible person?
* Are you planning your taxes with your CPA?
* Are you filing your taxes at three levels: federal, state, and city?
* Do you have a *good* CPA for advice?

22. Annual Reports:

(These are mandatory reports to be filed at the year-end.)

* Is your corporate book updated?
* Have you sent out annual payroll filings such as W-2, 1099, 941, 940, and NYS 45?

23. Credit Rating:

(Maintaining good credit both at the corporate and the personal level is necessary to get funding from outside sources.)

* Do you pay your bills on time?
* Do you bounce your checks?
* Do you check your credit reports from all the three agencies?
* Are you registered with Dun & Bradstreet to give you a rating in the industry?
* Do you have a good FICO score? (www.annualcreditreport.com)

24. Marketing/Advertising:

(Planning as to how to make your product or service available to the ultimate customer)

- Listing in various directories
- Flyers
- Newspapers
- TV and radio advertising
- Memberships in various organizations
- Pricing strategies
- Distribution of your products/services
  - ❖ Retailer
  - ❖ Professional selling
- Internet selling:
  - ❖ Do you have an interactive website?
  - ❖ Is it geared to sell?
  - ❖ Is your website linked to other websites?

Response to Self-Talk

- Self-talk: ***Why should I give up a secure job to chase a dream?***

Response: "Why would I stay in a job where an employer controls my fate when I could have the security of controlling my own future?"

Yes, I am probably giving up steady paycheck for the uncertainty of entrepreneurship. The flip side is that there is no secure career with any established company. I am a mere number. I could be laid off in the next wave of mergers or downsizing. I could be passed over for raises and promotions.

The fact is that my income may be irregular for a while, but I do not want to spend my life working for others when I could be achieving much more if I am on my own. So the greater risk is in not starting a business.

Alternate response: "Who said I was leaving my job?" I can launch a business in my spare time and leave my jobs only when the business is on the way to success.

- Self-talk: ***Why are you trying to launch a business when you should be trying to find a job?***
Response: "Launching a business could help me find a job."

If I am unemployed due to layoff or otherwise, I need an edge in the job hunting process. If I start a business, I have a better way to get a foot in the door.

I can get leads through business contacts and get opportunities to meet new people. Such meetings can lead to job offers.

Many employers are entrepreneurs themselves, making them predisposed to hiring other entrepreneurial types.

Launching a business also avoids having a period of unemployment in your work history. Fairly or not, employment gaps are red flags for many potential employers.

- Self-talk: ***I am too old to start a business.***

Response: "My decades of experience and business contacts are pluses, not minuses."

My age will more likely work for me than against me. I know the industry players better than the younger upstarts.

Working for myself now gives me more opportunity, as my job growth will be limited due to age.

Reality: Starting in 2014, under Obamacare, self-employed people will be able to obtain relatively affordable health insurance through new insurance marketplaces. Until now, individual health insurance could be very expensive or difficult to obtain for self-employed people who were older than fifty and/or who had health problems.

- Self-talk: ***I have heard that most new businesses fail.***

Response: "According to whom?"

Some daunting statistics are floating around about the failure rate of new businesses. You might hear that more than half fail in the first year. But such statistics are deceptive. Many of those failed new businesses actually were just hobby businesses that were never meant to last long or provide more than a few extra dollars on the side.

What's the true failure rate for new businesses? It's tricky to measure, but figures compiled by the Small Business Administration suggest that about 70 percent of new firms last at least two years, and about half last five years or more. Even those numbers significantly overstate the failure rate. Some of the new businesses that didn't last didn't fail. They closed because the entrepreneurs who launched them accepted attractive job offers, identified even better business opportunities or sold out to larger companies.

- Self-talk: ***My previous business failed. Will I succeed this time?***

Response: "The fact that I've tried before increases my odds of success."

Previous business failures aren't signs that I shouldn't try again. They're signs that I already have paid my dues learning hard lessons about entrepreneurship. Those lessons should serve me well this time around. I am now so much closer to success.

- Self-talk: ***This isn't a good time to be starting a business. The economy still is too unsettled.***

Response: "Times of economic uncertainty are great times to launch a business."

Consumers and businesses reevaluate their spending habits during unsettled economic times such as these. That reevaluation makes them more open to working with a new company—particularly one that offers good value.

Reality: Blue-chip companies launched during weak economics include FedEx, General Electric, General Motors, Microsoft, Procter & Gamble, and Walt Disney.

- Self-talk: ***No one will want what I am selling.***

Response: "How would I know?"

Is the person making this criticism one of my potential customers? Let me get more realistic feedback from people I actually intend to sell to.

- Self-talk: ***What do I know about starting and running a business?***

Response: "I know plenty about the sector I'm entering, and I can learn what I need to know about business. That's the easy part."

It is fair for critics to raise this issue if you haven't started and run a business before—being an entrepreneur does require some basic business skills. But these skills can be acquired relatively quickly. Josh Kaufman's book *The Personal MBA* (Portfolio) and John Jantsch's *Duct Tape Marketing*, blog (DuctTapeMarketing.com/blog) are great places to start.

- Self-talk: ***I can't afford to start a business.***

Response: "So I will start it on the cheap."

It can be very pricey to enter the manufacturing sector or even the retailing sector if your business idea requires an extensive inventory and/or a storefront. But there are plenty of business ideas that can be launched for just a few thousand dollars or less.

Examples: I can start an online business or a consulting business.